ELDER SPEAK
Journey to Wisdom

When an elder dies, a library burns to the ground.

~ AFRICAN PROVERB

ELDER SPEAK
Journey to Wisdom

Deb Pobst & Theresa D-Litzenberger

ISBN: 979-8-9858222-2-9 paperback

ISBN: 979-8-9858222-3-6 ebook

Cover design by Barbee Teasley

Editing by Morgan Fraser

Book Design by Damonza

FIRST EDITION

Printed in the United States

www.theripplefoundation.org

Contents

To Our Elders

Foreword

This Elder Speak manual will take you on a deep, rich, and rewarding journey. It is a guided journey that includes the Elder, their family and friends, the Elder Speak Program facilitators and, eventually, the greater community.

Elder Speak is a program born from the desire to listen to the stories and understand the too often untapped wisdom of Elders. Birthed from the creative genius and passionate efforts of Deb Pobst and Theresa D-Litzenberger, Elder Speak has evolved into a powerful and supported journey that reveals the "Inner Elder". In this revealing of the "Inner Elder" there is an opportunity for both an expression of and an affirmation of one's greatness. There is an owning of wisdom.

Elder Speak is one path of growing old that gives heart and soul to what it means to become an Elder.

So, what is an Elder? An Elder is, traditionally, someone who is old. But then we must ask, "Is every old person an Elder?"

We can talk about the semantics and dictionary definitions of *Elder* and *Old,* but for me, it comes down to one thing. I invite you to try this for yourself-

Take a moment and say, "I am an Elder."

Or "he is an Elder."

Now say to yourself "I am old."

Or "she is old."

Did you notice a difference?

That difference is the felt sense of the Elder archetype. The Elder archetype clearly carries more strength, resilience, respect, wisdom and even an aura of reverence.

This is an important distinction. It is this important distinction that comes alive in the Elder Speak program. Not all old people are Elders. Not that they couldn't be. Sometimes it takes an invitation, a reflection of value, a little encouragement, and guide to lead the way.

This Elder Speak manual is such an invitation.

This Elder Speak manual offers each one of us an opportunity to see, affirm and discover the "Inner Elder". The "Inner Elder" you discover may reside in your family, your neighborhood, or your community. And as you travel through this manual, you will also come to realize that deep within each one of us there is an "Inner Elder". Perhaps just waiting. Waiting for an invitation to take the journey.

Steve Stroud
Executive Director
The Ripple Foundation

Introduction

Elder Speak: The Journey to Wisdom

*The journey to wisdom can only be achieved through the
thoughtful integration of life experience.*

~ STEVE STROUD

Elder Speak is a program of two parts. The first part is a Personal Journey, offered to Elders, that guides them toward the wisdom of their life experience. The second part is the Elder Speak Community Event, where their wisdom is shared and celebrated.

Elder Speak began in 2015, when we were asked to create a program that would allow Elders to explore their wisdom by looking deeply at their life experiences. At the same time, we heard from young people in their 20s yearning for grandparents who could share their experience and wisdom to help with life decisions. We had stumbled onto a yearning that came from the young and the old; a yearning for wisdom. The Elder Speak Program was born of these requests.

The goal of this manual and the accompanying film is to help you create an Elder Speak Program in your own community. There is a great need for the sharing of the life experience and wisdom that is carried by our Elders. The Elder Speak Program meets that need.

The journey of Elder Speak is one of taking away layer upon layer of the dust and grime that cover the Elders' life experiences. Through repeated exploration from the questions asked, an Elder remembers long-forgotten details, including emotions, people, thoughts, and related experiences. The outcome of the exploration shifts from bare bones reliving until the essence of it gleams: it is the golden nugget; the wisdom piece hidden in the story. This is what the Elders share at the Elder Speak Community Event. This sharing of wisdom strengthens our communities.

This manual is divided into two sections to reflect the two parts of the overall program, in addition to an appendix with added resources to help with the planning and execution of your own Elder Speak Program.

Elder Speak Companion Film

This film by Eric Link—musician, videographer, and high school media arts teacher at Wenatchee Valley Technical Center—is a companion to the Elder Speak manual. It brings insight to the processes of interviewing Elders in such a way that their wisdom begins to reveal itself. We hope this film inspires you to embark on the Journey to Wisdom with the Elders of your community.

To view the Elder Speak Manual Video, search "Elder Speak Manual Video" on YouTube.
You can also view the Elder Speak Manual Video using this online link:
https://tinyurl.com/3eawuuhh

Part 1

THE PERSONAL JOURNEY

Finding Wisdom

From out one's soul is
Pulled the tissue
Of life, deep bound,
Though each day a
Flutter of wisdom's fabric,
A rustle, a breath…
What then is so
Wordlessly whispered?
Ah, that is
What must be
Attended to,
What must be
Deciphered, what
Must be caught in
The heart's mesh
And slipped on
Like a silken Robe

~Jana Sparks

Lesson 1

Finding the Elder

Everything comes from somewhere.

~ Nancy Gradwohl

You may be wondering how to actually find Elders that will enjoy the Elder Speak Program and bring the wisdom and depth of life experience you seek. Finding an Elder to participate can be fun and surprising. It always provides an opportunity to get to know someone new.

We include four Elders for each year's program. Even with these few participants, we may meet with up to eight or more people before we find those Elders interested in joining. Sometimes, it feels as if the Elders find us. Somehow, it always seems that the final four Elders share something in common; this commonality creates a theme for the group for the entire year.

Throughout the years of facilitating this program in our own community, we have found ways to make this process easier. This lesson will give you some insight into what steps to take for your own program.

Ask for suggestions from your friends and family members. Friends and family are a comfortable resource for finding an Elder. You are looking for an enthusiastic response from the person you asked. For example, "Oh, you have to ask___, he's lived such an interesting life and is just a great guy. I'd love to hear more about his life." This, coming from a friend or family member, is a good place to start.

If friends and family aren't able to help, there are many resources within the community. There may be groups of retirees that meet already, such as writing groups or hiking groups. The director or activities coordinator of a senior center may know of an Elder or two who might be interested in the program.

There are also many possibilities at assisted living centers. Each year, we have found terrific Elders from our local Senior Living Center who benefitted from the program and whose participation benefitted the community.

People who contribute within the community, such as participating in service clubs, on boards or in education, may also be great options.

Remember, Elders that have contributed to their community often stand out. You may see them on a local TV program, read about them in the newspaper, or hear a story about them on the radio. All these paths can lead you to the ideal Elder for your program. Write down the name of each Elder that interests you. If contact information is offered, you have what you need. If it is not offered, you may have to find another way to contact the Elder or find another Elder. Lesson 3 provides different options for contacting Elders. Trust that the right Elders will come. With patience and perseverance, you will soon have the people you need.

Now that you have a name or an idea of who you might ask to participate in the Elder Speak Program, you are ready for the next step.

❧

The Journey

This was our first Elder Speak and the first meeting with our selected Elders. Two of the Elders came. Theresa and I met an hour early and spent the time drinking tea and calming our nerves, excited to actually meet with Harriet and Beth. Beth arrived first. Friendly and outgoing, she reminded me of Mom P., my feisty red-haired mother in law. Something about this generation is uniquely different from women today. Very proper and yet not afraid to speak their mind. Harriet soon arrived and we began with some pointed questions, not from us but from her. "Why would young people want to come to this? Are they interested in old people? I didn't like old people when I was young." She then went on to point out a grammatical error on the handout I'd created, which we fixed on the spot.

Theresa gave an overview of the program and again questions came. "Is there entertainment?" No, we replied. This is from the heart, we want to create a forum where all speak from the heart, listen from the heart and are able to be spontaneous. "So we're the entertainment." Oh, so to the point.

Somehow the idea of entertainment brought the conversation around to music and memories began to flow. Harriet remembered the gramophone that played at breakfast every morning in her home; her favorite piece, L. Mozart's *Symphony for Children*. Beth remembered playing the triangle in early grade school to her favorite piece, *In a Chinese Temple Garden*. Both were absolutely glowing as they shared these memories and we were entranced.

All agreed that music and possibly animals are great ways of connecting generations. As the memories continued to flow about their life experiences, we realized that this was it. This was the connecting force we were hoping to find, and it flowed out naturally as they reminisced.

Lesson 2

Choosing Elders

Practicing sound work ethics will assist in achieving your career goals.

~ *Jim Wills*

Several criteria are important for finding Elders for the Elder Speak Program. In this chapter, you will learn all you need to select the best people who represent your community and are able to share their wisdom in an engaging way. When considering Elders for your program, it's a good idea to choose people who will benefit from the program, and whose experiences will be beneficial for the community to hear. We accept Elders in their mid-70's and older.

Qualities

In the beginning, as you bring Elder Speak to a community that is not familiar with the program, it is helpful to select Elders that are well-known to the community. These Elders will bring interest simply because they are known, loved and appreciated. This is a great way to introduce the program. As the community begins to understand the Elder Speak Program for what it is, you can bring any Elder forward, well-known or not, and there will be an audience ready to appreciate their Journey to Wisdom at your community event.

Below we will take a deeper look at the prospective Elder's health, computer skills, willingness to participate, curiosity, sense of service, and humor and talk about how these characteristics can contribute toward your decision.

Health

At the heart of it, being healthy allows the Elder to meaningfully participate in and attend meetings, in addition to the final community event.

The health of any Elder is important. Good health ensures each Elder has a positive experience and thrives. The Elder Speak Program can last nine months to a year and there are many long meetings. Each Elder needs the stamina to sit for two or three hours at a time and remain alert. Additionally, each Elder needs to clearly communicate with other people within the group and with the community. It is also helpful when an Elder can remember short-term and long-term memories. A healthy Elder can attend most—if not all—of the meetings throughout the year, in addition to the final event.

Activity

Elders who are active and show a variety of interests thrive in the Elder Speak program. They are interested in life outside of themselves. They are curious and always learning new things. Elders who enjoy engaging with others and with new experiences attract others to them.

Skills

Basic computer skills are extremely helpful. The use of email for communication is an important aspect. It is difficult to arrange meetings, ask and answer questions if the Elder does not have access to email. Although it can be done using phone calls and the postal service, be aware that doing it this way will take much more of your time.

Meetings by Zoom became mandatory during the COVID-19 pandemic when we could no longer meet in person. Zoom became a workable solution to keep the program going, even though we all would have preferred to meet in person. This is a personal decision you will make as you build your program. Sometimes a helper can connect the Elder, read the emails, etc. There are many creative ways to accommodate an Elder if you want to make it possible for him or her to participate.

Willingness

Not every Elder we ask to participate says yes. Not all are willing. The Elder who participates must be willing to be seen and heard by their community as they present what they have discovered about themselves and their life wisdom at the final community event. They must have the curiosity and the willingness to say yes to this new adventure, where they will deeply explore their past experiences and find their relevance in the present. They must be willing to share meaningful memories, even the painful ones. They must be willing to listen to others in the group and honor their experiences.

Service

A desire to be of service, to connect with community, and a sense of humor; these are the aspects of the type of spirit we look for in Elders. This work requires courage and vulnerability from the Elder. A sense of humor and some lightness of spirit can make all the difference in the process.

With these criteria in mind, follow your heart and ask the Elders who fit your criteria and see what happens. There is a lot of surrender in this process. Trust that the group that forms will be the one most needed for you, the Elders, the program and the community. Just keep looking and asking until you have four Elders who have said yes!

Once you have selected the Elders, it's time to take the next step: introducing the Elders to one another and forming the group.

⧸

The Journey

Rachel joined us a little late in the program. One of the Elders we had originally asked experienced debilitating depression and did not feel confident she could participate throughout the entire year. A friend recommended Rachel. She was a small, wiry, 90-year-old firecracker who was mostly blind and extremely deaf. She was tremendously interested in participating and hoped to contribute to the program.

Rachel enriched us all. She had a full life from which to draw experiences, and she shared them with laughter, warmth, and generosity. We learned to speak loudly for her. Best of all, we got to share her delight for life. Rachel's wisdom was to not take herself too seriously.

Lesson 3

Contacting the Elder

Things don't always go as planned. You have to accept change.

~ Jan Wallick

IN THIS EXCITING and often sensitive state of your process you begin to invite the Elders to join the Elder Speak Program. Keep in mind that the Elders may not know you or be familiar with the program. Great respect for this fact is required. Often, we feel shy about calling someone out of the blue. Once, someone suspected the call was a scam. In this lesson we will share how we have found success in making contact.

Here are the ways to effectively connect through friends and family, through your community, and through a media connection. Of course, if you already know the Elder you want to ask, you are set. You can call or email directly to arrange a meeting to tell them about your program.

When friends or family suggest someone, ask them to introduce you and Elder Speak to the Elder. Additionally, find out the easiest way to contact the Elder. Having the best means of contact with an Elder facilitates a straightforward conversation about Elder Speak. Sometimes, meeting an Elder for the first time with the friend or family member can smooth the first interaction. That friend or family member will know what is important to the Elder and be able to present the program to them in an appealing way.

When you receive information about an Elder through community resources, once again, find out the handiest means of contacting the Elder. You can go to where the Elder volunteers, or you can visit the senior center the Elder attends. If you visit with the director of the senior center, leave your contact number or email information with him or her so they can give it to the Elder, and respectfully ask for the Elder to get in touch with you.

Another option is to call or email the Elder to set up an in-person visit. If you are listening to an interesting Elder who is speaking at an event, introduce yourself afterwards and ask if you can call, meet, or exchange emails.

When you learn about an Elder through the media, such as a newspaper article, radio or TV show—or even social media—look for clues that may help you find a way to get in touch with the Elder. It may be as simple as contacting the media source to find the information you need. Because of privacy laws, this may not be possible, but it is worthwhile to ask. Share your reason for asking and leave your contact number with the media outlet. The Elder can then contact you if they're interested.

It is important that the Elders know they can get in touch with you if they would like to learn more about what you are offering. As your program grows, Elders will begin to know others who have gone through the program and enjoyed it. The program begins to have a reputation and it becomes easier to find willing Elders to participate. Elders from previous programs are extremely grateful for the opportunity to have participated.

Now that you have contacted interested Elders, it is time to introduce yourself and the program.

∽

The Journey

Everett was recommended to us by the local senior center director. We learned from the director that Everett participated in a writing group at the senior center, so rather than cold call him on the phone or through email, we attended his writing group, which was open to anyone. It was held in a large room. The participants sat at tables so they could write notes as they listened to others share their latest piece of writing. The tables were arranged in a large rectangle so that everyone could see each other. It gave an opportunity to get a feel for Everett in a group and to find out what kind of person he seemed to be. Afterwards, we introduced ourselves, explained our reason for attending, and talked about the Elder Speak Program. We gave him a handout introduction to the program. We exchanged contact information so that we could talk more after he had a chance to read the material.

Everett went on to enjoy the program despite health challenges. Afterward, his family expressed deep gratitude for the enrichment the Elder Speak Program brought to Everett and to the entire family.

Lesson 4

Introducing Elder Speak to the Elder

Well nurtured relationships are a most meaningful and rewarding part of life.

~ SUZANNE MCPHERSON

IN THIS LESSON, we give examples of how to introduce yourself and the Program to a prospective Elder by phone, by email, or through a friend or family member.

We have found that introducing ourselves and the Elder Speak Program with an open heart and an open mind makes all the difference. If you do this, the Elder will find it easier to do the same. As you visit, everyone will be more comfortable, open to hearing each other, and perhaps open to new adventures.

By Phone

When your introduction is by phone, begin with your name and explain that you are putting together a program called Elder Speak, a program that respects and honors local Elders. Tell them who recommended them and why you think they would be a wonderful addition to the program. Give more details about what the Elder Speak Program is and answer any questions they have.

Some example details are: They will be part of a group of four Elders going through this program together. It is a yearlong commitment with a public event the following September which they must attend. They will meet biweekly either in person or online, unless they need to skip a day or two. They will be filmed and interviewed by students who will create a film for the Elder Speak Community Event.

Suggest that you meet—within a week if possible—to explain more about the program. This gives them time to think about it and come up with any questions they may have.

By Email

Contacting an Elder through email is another way to introduce yourself and the program. An email is a more impersonal way of meeting someone, and yet, it gives an Elder time to think about answering. Your email introduction is the same as the one for a phone introduction. Keep it simple, and straightforward. Request that you meet by phone, Zoom, Skype, or in person.

Through Friends and Family

Introducing yourself through friends or family is slightly different. Ask your friend or family member to talk to the Elder about you and to explain a little bit about Elder Speak. Ask them to share something they have enjoyed about the program. The goal is to get permission from the Elder so you can contact them. This can be by phone, email, or in person.

In Person

If you are lucky enough to have your first contact and introduction happen in person, follow the same approach as given above for phone or email. Bring materials, printouts, or whatever you have that the Elder can take home and read. Set up a second meeting if the Elder needs time to think about making a commitment.

After all your effort, you may find disinterest, fear of getting involved, or a general confusion about the Elder Speak program. Some Elders do not feel they have anything to offer. Some feel it will be too much work. Some feel a pressure to perform. The Elder may not be interested enough to meet with you to talk more and could say no to joining the program.

You may have a strong sense that this Elder would be great for the program, but sometimes it is during the meeting that you will finally know for sure if they fit your criteria. If you decide during your meeting that the Elder will be unable to meet the rigors and demands of the Elder Speak Program, be honest about this. It is a demanding program at times. It requires an active, curious mind. It also requires emotional and physical stamina and a willingness to delve deeply into their life experiences.

The Journey

Someone recommended a highly respected and successful businessman as a potential Elder, so we met him at the local public market for coffee and tea. We spent at least an hour explaining the Elder Speak Program, letting him get to know us. We, in turn, learned about his history, not only as a businessman in the area, but about his past as well. He took home the pamphlets, flyers and information about the program and met with us again about two weeks later. At this meeting, he talked openly and genuinely about the effect of his mother's influence on his life, as well as other deeply personal reflections that came to him while thinking about doing the program. He understood the depth that the program could bring him.

Then he said no. He was not going to participate. He was afraid that people in the community would see him in a deeply personal light, and he did not want to be seen that way. He wanted to keep his persona as a successful businessman and a highly capable member of a prestigious board of directors. Additionally, he had recently promised his wife he would not volunteer for anymore events or programs so that they would have more time together. Though we were disappointed, we soon realized that even a "No" can reveal a sense of wisdom.

Lesson 5

Meeting the Elder

Living requires Courage! There are two types of Courage… physical and moral.
Strive daily to live by traditional values/virtues with a generous 'dose' of
Faith and Hope…and Humor. Physical courage will follow as needed.

~ *Mae Hamilton*

Once you have introduced yourself and the Elder Speak Program, arrange to meet to talk more about the experience of the Journey to Wisdom. This is an exciting time of face-to-face contact, and some guidelines can support your experience.

Meetings can be online using a platform like Zoom or Skype, or in person.

Sometimes, meeting in person is not possible for various reasons. When meeting online, arrange to meet at a time that works easily for you both and let the Elder know the meeting will last about 30 minutes to an hour. Use an online platform that the Elder knows and can join with comfort. We have found most people are familiar with Zoom and that they find it easy to use. If they aren't familiar with it, perhaps a friend or family member can help. Send the Elder the link to the meeting by email and follow up with a phone call or email the day before the actual meeting. If they are unsure of how to use the platform, offer to practice getting onto the Zoom call with them. On the day of your meeting, have your phone handy in case they have trouble so you can call and help them get connected. This meeting time is for introducing yourself in more depth, explaining more about the Elder Speak program, and hearing and answering any questions. If you haven't met in person already, it is also an opportunity to arrange for an in-person meeting.

Whenever we meet with Elders in person for the first time, we prepare material that an Elder can take home to read later. This may be pamphlets about your organization, the wisdom worksheet, or a program from the previous year. We have found a neutral meeting place like a café can support a feeling of safety. Having a cup of tea or coffee can give a sense of comfort. Another safe-feeling place for an Elder may be in the home of the friend or family member who suggested the Elder as a candidate.

Sometimes, an Elder just wants you to meet in their home. Once again, you are providing information, answering questions, and introducing yourself and the program more in-depth.

Introducing the Elder Speak Program means being clear about any expectations. If you are doing this program for the first time and you are still formulating that for yourself, you can explain what your hopes for the program are. This may be a hope of bringing Elder wisdom into your community. Or it may be connecting Elders more deeply with their community and creating relationship. Connecting generations to one another is another possibility.

Mostly, Elders want to know what is expected from them. The Elder Speak Program expectations are meeting once or twice monthly, exploring life experiences, looking deeply at them and discovering the wisdom that developed from these experiences. It also means identifying life tools that evolved from these experiences. They will present this Journey to Wisdom at a final community event.

Give the Elder any written material you prepared that they can keep and look at later. Along with the expectations and written material, provide anecdotes of past programs, tell how the program has impacted the community, and share how it impacted you.

Let them know that you will be there with them throughout the journey. Make sure they know that you will be at their side each step of the way. Explain your role as a facilitator and hold an openhearted and open-minded attitude. Listen deeply to whatever they have to say. Let them begin to experience what you are offering in this program.

Your goal is to provide a place where they can safely express themselves and explore their lives: a place where their highest qualities are reflected to them; a place where they can be vulnerable and understood. We acknowledge that we do not know their wisdom but that we trust their wisdom. During our conversation, we will often point out the wise statements the Elder makes during our first meeting.

We engage with laughter, too. Finally, we express ourselves as transparently as possible. As we practice our facilitation role, we show respect for the Elder and honor their needs. After all, the Elder Speak program is about the Elder.

᪾

The Journey

The first Elder we approached to participate in an Elder Speak Program was Harriet Bullitt. Harriet has been an entrepreneur, publicist and philanthropist. She created Sleeping Lady Resort and Icicle Creek Center for the Arts in Leavenworth, WA. We sat down on a cold January afternoon at O'Grady's Pantry on the Sleeping Lady campus over tea. After we explained the Elder Speak idea, she said, "No one wants to listen to old people. I certainly didn't. Who would come?"

Really? We thought. *You don't think people would want to listen to you?*

This is a common doubt that creeps into our Elder's decision to join. The other is this: to a person, every Elder says, "I don't have wisdom." They say it as a statement of fact and believe in its truth. What we discovered, and what we share with each Elder, is that we all have wisdom. We embody it from our experiences. The Journey to Wisdom is finding the lessons that are learned and lived from our life experiences.

In our first program year, we recognized that Elders firmly embody their wisdom even when they are unaware of it. Through the Elder Speak Journey, Elders become engaged with their own wisdom and learn how to express and share it with others. The journey that year took all five Elders confidently to the stage to tell their stories and share their wisdom. This is the essence of Elder Speak.

Lesson 6

What if the Potential Elder Isn't a Good Fit?

Accept yourself as you are and if there are parts you struggle to accept, hold these parts with compassion.

~ JANA SPARKS

YOU MAY INITIALLY have a strong sense that an Elder is great for the program and then discover that the rigors and demands of the Elder Speak Program are too much for them. The program requires an active, curious mind, as well as emotional and physical stamina to delve deeply into many life experiences. In this lesson, we explore how to communicate with an Elder when you suspect that he or she will be unable to fully participate in the journey.

It's best to determine, at the beginning of your interview process, if the Elder fits well into the program you have envisioned. The job of the facilitator is to decide; "Is the Elder comfortable joining the program?" If they express many concerns about trying to meet the requirements, reflect those concerns back to them and suggest that this may not be the time for them to join. Listen to what they tell you and do not push or pull them along. At the same time, support and encourage those who have doubts about their self-worth. Low self-worth is different from poor health, dementia, or not having time to commit to the program.

As you approach this with your open heart, use kind, honest, and compassionate language. As you listen to what the Elder says about their problems or hesitations to join or continue, repeat back to the Elder what you hear them saying. Together, you can decide whether this is a good fit for the Elder at this time. One of the things we have learned in our journey with the Elders is that they want transparency and honesty.

When Personal Crisis Occurs During the Journey

There are personal events that can happen during the journey that make it difficult or impossible for the Elder to continue. These can include failing health, death of a spouse, or an Elder moving away.

Remember, your commitment is to the Elder first. It is important to support them in any way you can if they are struggling for any reason. If they need to quit for the sake of their health, accommodate them and make it clear that you understand and support their decision.

Some of the accommodations may include: having a son or daughter step in at the final community event to represent the Elder whose health has failed; allowing the Elder to read his or her wisdom piece if dementia has worsened and they are not able to recall what they want to share; creating support within the group for the person if their spouse has died.

❦

The Journey

In my twenties, agonizing over a turning point decision in my life, I sought advice from my Grandmother rather than my mother. Her far reaching perspective seemed just what I needed; not to mention, I suspected my mother wouldn't approve of me changing direction, so this felt safer, too. After we talked a long time, and I heard her stories and her thoughts and her advice, her final parting words to me were, "And someday, you and your mother will get along, again, and you will listen to her, too."

She was right, of course, even though that wasn't what I wanted to hear.

That's the beauty of Elders speaking. Elders I know speak the truth from years of sorting out what is true and what isn't true. And by age 80 or 90, Elders are wise enough to say, "I don't know" when they don't know. Elders carry a history of experience that applies to today in uncanny and comforting ways. The human experience spans generations beyond my expectations.

Lesson 7

Coming Together

A full life is all about the relationships.

~ DAVE NOTTER

IN THIS LESSON, we explore how to create a cohesive group: a group in which strangers become friends who support each other through the Elder Speak Journey. We may start the Elder Speak Journey with seemingly little in common. However, there are three common threads that connect all of us to our shared journey: the sharing of life experiences; the recognition of wisdom; and the Elder Speak Community Event.

The First Group Meeting

First, set up a time and place for the whole group to meet. This meeting will include the four Elders and any facilitators; we usually have two to three facilitators for each group. We recommend meeting in person, in a quiet place where it is easy to hear each other. This can be a café, a person's home, a restaurant, or a tea shop. Wherever you decide to meet, be sure it is comfortable, easy to hear each other, and somewhat private so you can visit, laugh, and get to know each other with ease. A cup of tea or coffee and a cookie doesn't hurt, either. Gathering around a table is a good place to start building a cohesive group. If you cannot meet in person, arrange a Zoom or Skype meeting and go from there.

Begin by introducing yourself and each of the facilitators. As you introduce the Elders, ask each one to say something about themselves. Allow each person to share briefly about their life to help establish familiarity with one another.

In any group, finding commonality is helpful. The easiest way to find common threads is by listening to each Elder tell their stories. Often, one Elder's story sparks memories from others in the group. Sometimes, a question comes up. Sometimes, the story sparks a discussion. You can engage the Elders by supporting the discussion with your own questions that invite further exploration. The more discussion, the more common threads are discovered. Anytime you notice common experiences, reflect them back to the group. This will help them recognize their similarities.

Notice who speaks readily and who doesn't. Make openings for each Elder to have a chance to speak.

Listen carefully to any questions someone may have about the journey they are about to take. Answer their questions as transparently as possible. Listen for any doubts or concerns. This is an important time to learn about these concerns so that the group can explore ways to support one another. Honor the Elders for saying yes to this new adventure.

Before ending, set up a time and date for the next meeting and explore setting a future schedule of meetings. Decide which days and time work best for the group. We recommend meeting twice a month.

Give the Elders a handout with the facilitators' contact information, including both phone numbers and email addresses. Let them know they can call or email you anytime if they have questions. Get their contact information to create a contact list for everyone. Hand out the photo release form, as found in the appendix, to sign and collect later, and any other forms you need the Elders to complete. Request that they write a short biography of themselves to bring to the next meeting. Take a head shot photo of each person.

Now you have the beginnings of a cohesive group. Building rapport will take time, so trust the process and keep your hearts and minds open to the moment you are in. Enjoy the Elders and the journey you are embarking upon with them.

∽

The Journey

In one Elder Speak group, there was a mortician, a pastor, a doctor, and an orchardist, a diverse mixture of experiences and professions. One day we discussed how they respond to stress. They all found their common thread in their answers. Jim described himself as a happy individual who believes that starting the day with feeling positive helped him through the day. Nancy believed that every day is a choice in how one faces the day. While she does not ignore stress, she gathers herself together and asks herself how to approach it with positive action, prayer, and confidence in the future. Dave said his approach to stress is like Nancy's. He said stress is his sadness. He practices empathy. Sandy said she practices changing her attitude to ease her stress.

By finding the common thread of their stress and how they worked through it, they felt more cohesive as a group in their common human experience.

Lesson 8

Exploring the Meaning of Life Experience

God heard my prayer and took my despondency away.
I knew he would care for me the rest of my life.

~ CARL CAMPBELL

EXPLORING WISDOM GAINED from life experience is best achieved with regularly scheduled meetings. We suggest meeting with the Elders twice a month, every month, for the nine months that lead up to your scheduled community event. In this lesson, we discuss methods of delving into the Elders' stories and deepening their awareness of the wisdom they hold within these stories.

The facilitation and discussion process have been a long, humbling journey of learning for us. In our first Elder Speak, we were lucky to have Elders who mostly guided themselves as we dipped our toes into leading discussions. We continue to learn new skills as the Elder Speak Program grows and evolves.

You may or may not be comfortable with facilitating conversations and leading discussions. In this lesson, we will give you guidelines and suggestions to help develop these important skills.

We will look at how to create a safe and inclusive environment; active listening; witnessing; facilitating open discussion; facilitating flow and conversation; and acceptance. Each process deeply affects the group in a positive and lasting way.

Creating a Safe and Inclusive Environment

The goal of facilitation is to honor the Elder's life and experience. Facilitation is defined in the Cambridge Dictionary as: *the process of making something possible or easier.* For any of this to happen, first you must create a safe environment. In a safe environment everyone is seated comfortably, can speak and be heard without interfering noise, and can see one another easily. One of our Elders likened it to sitting at a round table. We often keep this in mind and invoke the spirit of the round table even if we are not at an actual table. At the 'round table', we are in a welcoming and friendly bubble where no one is judged. Anything that is spoken to the group is confidential unless the speaker says otherwise.

Facilitation Guidelines for Creating a Safe and Inclusive Environment

1. Be aware of yourself. Notice if you are comfortable, breathing easily and present in the moment. If you do not feel present or comfortable take a deep breath or two. Once you are comfortable, the others will be able to relax too. If you can't relax, name what you are feeling and share it with the group.
2. Expand your awareness to the whole group. Make eye contact and be aware of each person in the group. Ask yourself what they might need to feel safe.
3. Clarify the purpose of the days' gathering.
4. Explain the rules of engagement for this group.
5. Confidentiality: Everything is kept confidential within the group.
   a. Uninterrupted speaking: We allow each person to speak fully and will refocus that person only as needed.
   b. Open sharing: All experiences have great value. Encourage the sharing of all life experiences. If the person isn't ready to share let that be okay. Difficult experiences may naturally come out later as the person gets more comfortable with the program.
   c. Unconditional Support: Sometimes the journey to wisdom challenges us. Discomfort is a valuable part of that journey. As one Elder said, "It's okay to struggle." We support each person by holding their feelings and memories with respect and open hearts.

Active Listening

Once the Elders have met and begun to know each other, dedicate one entire meeting to each Elder so they can tell their life story in more depth. This means it will take four meetings to hear all four Elders' stories. You can prearrange the schedule so that each Elder knows when they will be telling their story. Give that Elder the floor and let them fully tell their story while they are witnessed by all the Elders and facilitators who are present.

This is a powerful experience.

Facilitation Guidelines for Active Listening

1. Active listening is focused listening where all your attention is on the speaker.
2. Active listening involves our body, mind and heart; using all our senses we model an open and accepting environment that invites authentic exploration.

3. When we actively listen with all our senses, we hear not only what the person says, we also hear what is implied.
4. By actively listening, we become curious and ask open-ended questions to bring the speaker deeper into their experience.
5. Active listening allows for a pause, a moment of silence, between what the speaker has said and how you may respond.

Witnessing

As the Elders tell their story, we are witnesses to their life. This may be the first time some aspects of the Elders' life have been told. As we listen and witness this, a sense of the sacredness of life often comes over the group.

Facilitation Guidelines for Witnessing

1. Witnessing is a nonjudgmental, openhearted state.
2. Witnessing the speaker is being fully aware of their physical, mental, and emotional states.
3. Witnessing ourselves is being fully aware of our physical, mental and emotional response to the speaker while the speaker is sharing their life story.
4. Witnessing increases your awareness to ask the questions that deepen the speaker's process.
5. Witnessing opens the group to a compassionate experience of each other's life stories. The grace of being witnessed brings a willingness to share more deeply within the group.

The Power of Open-Ended Questions

After each Elder tells their life story, we ask open-ended questions that require elaboration. Almost always, our questions relate to what we heard a person say or imply. The key to this is to first say what you think you heard the person say. For instance, you will begin your question by saying, "When you talked about your experience as a ten-year-old, I heard you say…"

Examples of Open-Ended Questions

- What were you feeling when that happened?
- What or who helped you in that situation?
- Where did your strength come from?
- How did this experience affect your life?
- Tell me more.

With open-ended questions you are providing an opportunity for the Elder to feel their feelings, remember their thoughts and to be the author of their experience. Now, the Elder stops *narrating* the story and begins *to live* the story. In these moments of living the story, the Elder rediscovers the meaning of the experience. By discovering the meaning, the Elder discovers their wisdom.

Facilitation Guidelines for Open-Ended Questions.

1. Allow each Elder to tell their story without interruption or judgment.
2. Reflect the potent aspects of each life experience. This reflection provides the Elder a chance to know how he or she thinks, feels, acts and to know they were heard.
3. Check to make sure that what you hear is what the Elder meant to say.
4. Reflect back the life wisdom you have heard in their story.

Facilitating Open Discussions

After this initial period in which the Elders tell their life stories, the meetings can have a different focus, becoming more of an open discussion format. In the open discussions, we like to create an atmosphere of friends and family sitting around the table. This can be done easily when meeting in person. If you are meeting by Skype or Zoom, ask each participant to visualize their favorite family table and see us meeting together there, gathered in a circle.

We ask the Elders to speak from their hearts and listen deeply to one another. We continue to use open-ended questions throughout our discussions. Elders may feel vulnerable as they share deeply, yet this is how they reach the wisdom contained in their stories.

Now you can bring forward any questions that you believe will open and deepen the experience of the group. Invite everyone to ask questions that come up as they listen to each other. One speaker's experience can spark memories in another. Find the similarities of experience that you heard in each story and ask a question that highlights the similarities. Delve deeper into something that stood out to you. Trust yourself.

This is often a confusing time for the Elders because they want answers about what they are supposed to do. The answer to that question is: this is the time to reflect on their lives to find the wisdom and the tools that helped them, to understand where those tools came from, and when they saw those tools used by others.

Ask the Elders for any questions they may have.

Facilitating Flow and Conversation

The flow in conversation builds trust in knowing that everyone has a voice and every voice matters. Conversation brings the group together by building shared experience.

Facilitation Guidelines for Flow and Conversation.

1. Redirect if an Elder is lost or rambling. You can do so by interjecting, "I hear you saying…" and naming the core essence of what you hear the speaker sharing.
2. If one Elder talks too much and the group is out of balance (others are drifting off or not able to get a word in) redirect by saying, "I notice that _____ has something to say."
3. As you listen and reflect back what you hear, ponder what you don't hear. Notice if there are unspoken questions, discomfort, shyness, or resistance to going deeper into an experience. You can name what you sense to open the group to more discussion. One example that can open the discussion is saying, "I'm sensing some discomfort in the group, is there something that we're missing?"

Acceptance

We encourage the Elders to accept all aspects of their life. Every experience has value, whether it's good or bad, painful or happy; all experience teaches us something. Allow experiences to be exactly as they are. Honor what presents itself. Whenever you can, involve everyone in the discussion. Allow opportunity for relating to one another's stories. Each person can share a similar experience, feeling, or thought on the matter. When it is appropriate, boldly share your own thoughts and feelings on the topic. Sometimes, your sharing opens others to a deeper reflection of their own thoughts and feelings.

You have now gone deeper into the life experience of the Elders and may be beginning to get glimmers of the wisdom they have gained from these experiences. Again, trust the process. It will take time and repetition for the Elders to begin to see beyond the story they know into the deeper story they have not yet seen. This deeper story is where the gift of wisdom lies.

One reward for being with Elders on their journey of deepening understanding into their life experiences is the rich and meaningful moment when an Elder says, "I had no idea Elder Speak would be like this. I am learning so much about my life, and about myself."

❧

The Journey

Deb's mother died soon after the Elder Speak program in 2018. That year, two of the Elders' spouse died and one of the Elders was diagnosed with an unexpected terminal illness. Deb wrote this for the monthly newsletter.

Transitioning from Daughter to Matriarch.

Transitioning from one role in life to the next can be so disorienting. Who am I now that my mother is gone? I'm the same person I was and yet I'm not. I've lost a certain piece of my sense of identity and I've yet to find the new sense of self that will replace it. I can't describe this missing piece.

I tried to name it daughter, but that didn't begin to fit the bigness of it. I thought about naming it love, but the love is still there, so that's not it. Friend? No.

I know this is grief, I understand that. I've recently looked to our Elders—Jim, Suzanne, Mae, and Everett—as they walk through huge losses of husband, wife, and health, wondering how they do it with such grace.

They describe getting up in the morning and making the bed. They call it an important first step. Make the bed, then coffee, and the day has begun.

Wisdom is often simple like that.

Profound and simple.

Lesson 9

Wisdom Worksheet

There is a difference between knowledge and wisdom.

~ Everett Burts

The Wisdom Worksheet is a tool that guides the user in finding wisdom from significant life events. It gives Elders the opportunity to explore events of different life stages, starting from birth to age 10, teenage years, and so on to current day. In this lesson we discuss the history of the Wisdom Worksheet, how it is used in the Elder Speak journey, and its benefits.

Rita Clark introduced us to the Wisdom Worksheet. She used it at her senior center and found it to be profound. Gratefully, we integrated it ourselves and have used it as a mainstay of the program ever since. Over time we modified it to fit our purpose; you can modify it for your purpose, too.

We pass out copies of the Wisdom Worksheet at the end of the first group meeting. We go over the worksheet together, answer questions and encourage a playful attitude while they fill it out.

WISDOM WORKSHEET

Reflecting on your childhood, let us say, up to about 10 years of age, can you pinpoint any experience (positive or negative) that left a significant impression on you?

_____

_____

What, if anything, did you learn from this experience that has lasted through your life or a major part of it?

_____

_____

Reflecting on your life as a teenager, can you identify any major experience (positive or negative) that left a significant impression on you?

_____

_____

Did any major learning occur because of this experience? If so, what was it?

_____

_____

Reflecting on your life roughly from 20-55, can you identify any major experience(s) that left a lasting memory?

_____

_____

What did you learn from this?

_____

_____

Identify any additional experiences that left major lasting impressions.

_____

_____

What did these experiences teach you?

_____

_____

Now review your learnings (**in bold print**) above, and see if you can synthesize some or all of them in one or two WISDOM STATEMENTS, and write it/them below

NOTE: Your WISDOM STATEMENT can be one or two short sentences.

Facilitation Guidelines for the Wisdom Worksheet

1. Do a Wisdom Worksheet yourself before asking the group to do one.
2. Explain that the early years of our lives shape our beliefs and behaviors the most.
3. Share that once the process of remembering begins, other Elders have experienced a cascade of memories long forgotten. They begin remembering people, events, and outcomes that sat like boxes in an attic, dusty and forgotten but full of precious moments.
4. Reaffirm that this is an exercise they can do over and over again as new memories surface.
5. Explain that each memory has value no matter how insignificant it seems.
6. Ask Elders to explore memories with a new perspective, to look at what the experience taught, and to notice how it changed the way they approached their lives.

After handing out the Wisdom Worksheet, let the Elders know that you are available to answer questions. Tell them that you will go over their answers as a group at the next meeting. This will continue for the rest of your journey together. They may or may not fill out the worksheets, but you will continue to bring it up, hand out new copies, and go over whatever is brought up by those who have filled it out. Use it as the basis for your discussions. As they rewrite the answers to the questions, new or more vivid memories flow. Even more, a pattern about themselves emerges. One person may discover he is always looking for the truth; another may find she is independent and strong; a third may see struggle as a way of life. It is from these findings that Elders discover the wisdom statement that guides them most in life.

We find it can be hard to tackle the Wisdom Worksheet. There is something vulnerable about searching for the deeper meaning of our life experience and looking for the wisdom in it.

We are traditionally taught to look for wisdom outside of ourselves: in our teachers, peers, books, and religions. These all can hold great wisdom and be of tremendous comfort and value. Looking inward does not replace the value of wisdom found outside of ourselves. Instead, it enhances it.

The Wisdom Worksheet offers the opportunity to look inward rather than outward; to find wisdom born of one's own life experience.

You will want to have the Elders' final wisdom statements in hand a month before the final community event so you can print them on the programs.

Now you are deep into the journey and ready to put together your final event.

❧

The Journey

Theresa wrote this for a newsletter.

Finding Grace in Wisdom

What is wisdom and how is it different from advice? One of the Elders participating in Elder Speak says that wisdom is knowing when not to give advice. At 91, she had only just discovered the difference when visiting her granddaughter and observing her lifestyle. Jane ached to offer advice for how her granddaughter could live more easily. Wisdom told her to keep her advice to herself, and more importantly, appreciate her granddaughter's place in life in that moment.

When I began struggling with my sense of growing older, I turned to the book, "The Gift of Years," by Joan Chittister. In her chapter on wisdom, she describes the period of elderhood as a service. "The service of elders is not a service of labor. It is a service of enlightenment, of wisdom, of discernment of spirits."

Is this true? I asked myself. Deb and I went to our Elders to ask for their experience with aging. We asked for their wisdom about it. First, to a person, they say, "I have no wisdom." But then, as their experiences are shared and the lessons learned are teased out—along with how these experiences and lessons informed their lives—the wisdom flows quickly and easily: a gift at the door; the golden nugget.

Wisdom is a very human experience since it is born from our experiences. Wisdom is that golden nugget that informs us in times of need. And if we have not had the experience, that

34

nugget can be learned from another who has had the experiences and lessons. When the time comes that I am amid a challenge, I can say, "Oh yes, one of my Elders experienced this. Here was her wisdom from it."

To learn these wisdom pieces, though, I need to be in conversation with my Elders. To receive what Joan Chittister calls "the ancient truth," I need to stop my busy life, sit down and be in connection with my Elders. And listen.

How do I find my own wisdom? Again, I need to stop my busy life, sit down with myself and listen. As I sit with an experience or a question, I take deep, calming breaths and focus on my heart. While focused this way, I hold gratitude for this moment, for this question, for this experience. In time, the wisdom floats into my awareness. I feel a full bodied and emotional connection to this wisdom. It is the golden nugget; the "ancient truth;" the final Aha.

Part 2

THE ELDER SPEAK COMMUNITY EVENT

*Wisdom
is a living stream,
not an icon preserved
in a museum.*

*Only when we
find the
spring of wisdom
in our
own life can it flow
to future generations.*

~THICH NHAT HANH

Lesson 10

Preparing for the Elder Speak Community Event

Without family, friends and community, what I believe in can become so one dimensional that my love of words, thoughts and ideas, my love of books and poetry, music and lyrics is worth no more than a hill of beans: sharing is everything.

~ PAT RUTLEDGE

THE CULMINATION OF the Elder Speak Journey is the Community Event. This is a production, held in a local venue once a year, where the Elders share their wisdom, stories and journey with their community. We usually hold our annual event in September, on Grandparents' Day. The Elders are on a stage; seen, heard, and honored by all who come. They in turn honor us with their courage, wisdom, and open-hearted sharing.

We asked ourselves, "How do we bring Elder wisdom into our community?" That was the question we held as we imagined the Elder Speak Program. We began to foresee an event at which Elders share their wisdom, stories and journey with an audience.

The event we created may look differently than the one you imagine. In either case, you may find some of our suggestions helpful with the planning and creation of your Elder Speak Community Event.

In these lessons we present, in chronological order, the steps we use to create the community event. We also present options and outline some of the choices you will need to make in order to create the event that best fits your needs.

Lesson 11

The Community Event
Preparation Timeline

There is nothing wrong with the struggle.

~ OTTO ROSS

THE FOLLOWING CHAPTERS will go into more detail about the various components of the Elder Speak Community Event. Here is a timeline we created for ourselves that you may also find useful. Some of the actions included in this timeline are discussed in greater detail in the lessons.

Elder Speak Timeline

October-December:
- Confirm Elders
- Meet and greet with Elders
- Hand out Wisdom Worksheet
- Schedule interviews of Elders with high school media arts class
- Film Elders at high school media arts class

January:
- Meet with Elders twice – start telling individual life stories
- Collect signed permission forms for photos
- Collect biographies

- Take individual photos
- Post about program/share about Elders on website
- Find venue for the Elder Speak Community Event and confirm date
- Begin securing financial sponsorships

February:

- Meet with Elders twice – complete telling individual life stories
- Secure financial sponsorships
- Contact newspaper and schedule interviews of Elders to start in May

March:

- Meet with Elders twice
- Begin general discussions with Elders
- Work with Wisdom Worksheets

April:

- Meet with Elders twice
- Continue general discussions with Elders
- Work with Wisdom Worksheets
- Check in with high school film class about progress of film
- Confirm the schedule of interviews dates and times with the newspaper

May:

- Meet with Elders twice
- Start to zero in on the Elders' wisdom statements
- Newspaper interview of first Elder takes place and is published in May
- Confirm in-kind donations of food and drinks for event
- Search for volunteers for the following aspects at the event:
    - Ushers
    - Registration table
    - Sponsor table
    - Food prep and service
    - Wine server
    - Donation jars
    - Mic runners
    - Flower arrangements
    - Help with set up and break down

June:

- Meet with Elders twice
- Continue zeroing in on the wisdom statements in discussions
- Newspaper interview of second Elder takes place and is published in June
- Reconfirm event venue, date and time

- Create save-the-date postcards
- Post on social media

July:

- Meet with Elders twice
- Continue zeroing in on wisdom statements in discussions
- Post event on social media
- Print save-the-date postcards, posters and flyers.
- If including flyers with Chamber of Commerce newsletter, arrange for this.
- Newspaper interview of third Elder takes place and is published in July
-

August:

Elders:

a. Meet with Elders twice
b. Confirm Elders' wisdom statements
c. Newspaper interview of fourth Elder takes place and is published in August
d. Hand out day-of-event schedule
e. Answer questions, support Elders in whatever way they need
f. Hand out save-the-date postcards to give to friends and family
g. Schedule a September practice date at venue

Staff:

a. Create two schedules of the day of event. One for Elders, one for staff.
b. Hand out day-of-event schedule to staff
c. Mail postcards at the beginning of the month
d. Put up posters and flyers toward the middle of the month
e. Post on social media once or twice a week
f. Email reminders to supporters
g. Meet with venue staff to confirm event needs
h. Print programs for event
i. Secure film from high school media class
j. Confirm volunteers
k. Confirm all in-kind donations
l. Schedule a practice run through with Elders in September at venue
m. Secure banquet permit

September:

Elders:

a. Rehearsal at the venue
   1. Seating arrangements
   2. Speaking order
   3. Review schedule of the day

    4. Speaking into microphones

    5. Practice talking to the audience and to one another on the stage

  b. Answer questions, support Elders in whatever way they need

Staff:

  a. Refine day of schedule, last minute changes, etc.

  b. Continue to post on social media and email people

  c. Call Elders the day before the event to check in and confirm the time they will arrive at the venue.

  d. Take student film to tech support at venue at least one day before the event

  e. Do whatever is necessary to prepare and decorate the stage for the event

Day of Event:

  a. Prepare/deliver refreshments

  b. Meet and greet volunteers before the event begins and answer any questions about their responsibilities

  c. Check in with tech support at venue

  d. Meet Elders and follow day of schedule

  e. Enjoy doing the event

  f. Clean up and break down after the event

After Event:

  a. Check in with the Elders

  b. Write thank you notes for any donations received

  c. Write thank you notes to sponsors

  d. Schedule a meeting with Elders to talk about the event and their experience

  e. Ask for any suggestions the Elders might have to improve the event

  f. Thank the Elders for taking this Heroic Journey to Wisdom

Lesson 12

Funding Options for Your Elder Speak Community Event

Love and honor your family; buy only what you need; invest wisely.

~ JANE HENSEL

OUR PROCESS BEGAN by imagining a free community event staffed by volunteers. The next step was understanding any costs that might be incurred and how to fund it.

Our Elder Speak Journey and Community Event are entirely volunteer driven. We receive in-kind donations for every aspect of the event, including staff time. There are some additional costs such as advertising (posters, radio, newspaper, TV) and program printing costs. Financial sponsorships from our local community have paid for these accrued costs.

Not every Elder Speak Journey and Community Event needs to be volunteer driven. If you are working for a non-profit or a business that provides activities for seniors, you can implement this program without it falling under the auspices of volunteerism. In either case, we have found that it takes about eight hours per week to run the Elder Speak Journey and the Community Event for the nine months leading up to the event.

We choose to volunteer because it enriches our lives beyond anything for which we could be paid. We love traveling with the Elders as they journey through their life experiences and find their wisdom. At the final Community Event, it is deeply rewarding to see the Elders humbly share their wisdom with community. It is in this moment we see them come full circle. By valuing their wisdom and life experience, they point the way for us to value our own wisdom and life experience. We are honored to be present at this intersection of our shared humanity.

Sponsors can provide support through in-kind donations or financial donations. An in-kind donation may be a sponsor that provides the venue, food, drink, promotion through advertising, articles in the newspaper or coverage on the radio free of charge. Some sponsors are financial. These sponsors are usually businesses that like to feel involved in the community through their financial donation to an organization.

Whichever sponsor you are talking or writing to, they all like to know who you are and your role in the event. They want to know its name and why it is important for the community. They want to know how much money or in-kind donation you need and why, and what recognition they will receive for their sponsorship.

Any organization that supports the community event is likely to be a strong supporter of your community. Give appreciation and recognition to all sponsors by putting their logos on all posters and your website. Mention them at the event itself.

Lesson 13

Bringing in Outside Support

A positive attitude and grateful spirit give peace.

~ *PATTY CHRISTENSEN*

IN THIS LESSON, we will explore outside resources that you may find in your community and give you suggestions on how to bring them in as supporters of your program.

While every community has its own unique flavor, there are assets that most communities share. These are the local newspaper, radio station, schools, senior center, library, churches and clubs. Finding the outside resources that will support your Elder Speak Program will most likely begin with these community assets.

Community support is invaluable for the Elder Speak Program. Advocates in the community provide complementary services that enrich the program.

Newspaper/Radio

If you have a local newspaper or radio station, contact them and explain what you are doing. Ask if they would be interested in doing interviews of each of your Elders, as well as interviewing you about the Elder Speak Program itself. These interviews can be timed to be published in the four months leading up to the Elder Speak Community Event, one elder per month, as a way to advertise and bring awareness to your event. Our local newspaper has written articles about Elder Speak for each year of the program. For some years now, the publisher, Rufus Woods, has interviewed each Elder for his podcast and for an article about each Elder. Elders are given the opportunity to review impactful times of their lives, answer questions that dive deeper into these experiences, and, in most cases, relive the moments emotionally as well as mentally.

Ask for permission to film the Elders while they are being interviewed. This gives you material that you can use on social media. You can take 1-to-3-minute clips from the interviews and post them on your social media profiles.

Senior Center, Library, Church, Clubs

These are great community hubs, and they will be interested in what you are offering. As they come to understand Elder Speak, they may offer things like a meeting space that you can use, or refreshments for your event. Say "yes" with gratitude to any offers of help that come your way.

Schools

If there is a videography class at a local school, college, or technical learning center talk to the teacher. Explore the possibility of having the class interview each of the Elders and create a film that can be shown at the Elder Speak Community Event. This has worked out beautifully for us and we have noticed that the Elders and students both benefit greatly from this collaboration.

In the first year, we contacted a local high school videography class. This class has interviewed and filmed each Elder individually for seven years now. It is part of the lesson plan to teach the students the art of the interview, filming the interview, and creating a short video of all the Elders as a final project.

This service benefitted both the students and the Elders. The Elders learned the feel of sharing their story and wisdom with others. The students learned videography skills while also hearing stories that amazed and inspired them. This class provided the Elders the opportunity to review impactful times in their lives and what each learned from those experiences. During the interview, the Elder shares a brief history of their life and some impactful memories or moments. Then he or she answers questions from the students and teacher. After the first half hour, the Elder forgets the camera and begins to share spontaneously. As questions from everyone become more personal, Elders discover emotions tied to the experience that they may have forgotten and share them with the class.

We limit the film the students create from the interviews to 15 - 20 minutes and show it at the beginning of the community event. It is very well received. Find what works for you and your community.

Lesson 14

Materials Needed from the Elders

The challenges and trials in life, can and have given me the ability to be grateful.

~ SANDY REIMAN

IN THE MEETINGS with the Elders, you will ask them for four things:

1. Biographies – simplified to 1 or 2 paragraphs
2. Permission to video/audio record and photograph them
3. Signed photo release form (Find the form in the appendix)
4. Their Wisdom Statement

Task #1 is to ask the Elders to write an autobiography for the website and promotion. This aids them in the process of recalling important life experiences and lets the community know who they are. They will use the Wisdom Worksheet to help jump-start their memories. We ask them to keep this simple and short. If it seems too long, ask for permission to edit as needed.

Task #2 and 3: take a head shot photograph of each Elder for the website and future promotions. Ask each Elder to sign a photo release form so that images, videos and interviews can be used freely. With these in hand, you have what you need to create materials for your program.

Task #4 is to ask the Elders to write a single wisdom statement that can be used on the event program. This is something the Elders work on throughout the year and is completed one month before the Community Event.

Lesson 15

Choosing a Venue

You have a choice, accept what you are given,
love greatly and happiness is for you to reach out and grab.

~ *PAT MOYER*

CHOOSING A VENUE can be based on many factors.

1. Does it meet the needs of the program you have in mind?
2. Does it provide enough audience space?
3. Does it allow for the Elders to be seen and heard easily?
4. Does it allow for the Elders to see and hear each other?
5. What is the cost?
6. Is it handicap accessible?
7. Does it have sufficient parking?

Elder Speak resonates with community-minded people and many will offer to help you. We were fortunate to be offered the use of our local performance arts theater. Consider finding the arts center in your community and see if they would be willing to support your event. If you do not have an arts center that is available, check out other community centers such as schools, the local senior center, churches or anyplace that has a large gathering space that you could use.

Once you have secured the venue, set the date and time. We have used Grandparents' Day successfully in the past: the first Sunday after Labor Day. However, eventually we changed to a later Sunday in September because of conflict with our local county fair. Check for other events happening in your area and choose a date that works best for you.

We find two hours to be a good length of time for the Elder Speak Community Event. Choose the time of day that you believe will bring the most participation from your community.

Lesson 16

Organizational Details

Stop talking and start listening.

~ Dennis Carper

Below are some of the details you'll need to consider and arrange before the community event itself. You may find your list is slightly different than ours, or that it will change over time as you discover what works best for you and your community.

Furniture

If your venue has a stage, you will want to create a setting for the Elders with an ambiance of some kind. We like to use a living room setting with a couch, armchairs, lamps, carpet, and accent tables. Another possibility is an outdoor setting of wicker chairs and side tables. Whatever you choose, you need to secure the furniture through rentals or donations and have it set in place the day before or the morning of the community event. Be aware of your Elders' needs as you select your chairs. It is best to use chairs or couches with firm seats that are easy to get in and out of. We have found it important to have some pillows available for the Elders, too. Check with your Elders for their specific needs before the day of the event so you can ensure their comfort.

Flowers

Flowers add life to the setting and brighten the mood. Local flower growers or flower shops may be happy to donate flowers for your event. Offer to come pick them up the day before to make sure you have the arrangements ready on time.

Water

Have water available for the Elders during the event. Fill glasses beforehand and have a water pitcher nearby. Use glasses that will not tip easily and are comfortable to use.

Food and Drinks

Before the event, to provide a welcoming setting for the audience, you have several options that depend on the layout of your venue and what your budget or donations allow. We like to create a meet-and-greet area in the foyer of the theater and serve water, coffee, tea and wine with finger foods. You can, of course, skip this and simply seat the audience as they arrive.

After the event, we gather and enjoy refreshments again. This is a time for audience members to mingle and visit with one another and the Elders. It's also a valuable time for connection among all who have come. This can be arranged with or without food and drink. Decide what fits your community and your budget.

A local winery may be willing to donate their wine and service to your event. Local grocers and businesses may donate food platters and cookie plates as well. See what your community has to offer. Give them sponsorship recognition on all advertising, as well as a grateful mention in your program.

Advertising

Advertising and promotion are an important aspect of the community event. We break this into two categories: free and paid.

Free Advertising Ideas

During the entire Elder Speak Journey, you will be promoting your event. Send out monthly news-letters that let your audience meet the Elders and follow their journey. Post interviews and snippets of film of the Elders on social media. As you get closer to your event, do radio interviews, or speak with your local television station about doing a piece about your program. You can potentially include interviews with the Elders in all of these scenarios. Give as much information as you can about Elder Speak to pique peoples' interest. Send all pertinent information about your event to the local newspaper.

If you have the support of a local newspaper reporter who has been willing to interview the Elders and write articles highlighting each Elder, check that these articles have been posted monthly during the last four months of your program.

Paid Advertising Ideas

In the three months prior to your Event, print and post flyers, posters and save-the-date postcards. Print enough postcards to mail them to your supporters. Give the Elders postcards for their family and friends.

Radio and newspaper advertising can be used to get the word out about your Event.

Promotional and Program Materials

In the months ahead of your event, create all program and promotional materials. Have a printed program ready to hand out to each audience member as they walk through the door. In the last few years, we put wisdom statements from each Elder on the back. We also added lined spaces for audience members to write down anything they want to remember, or a question to ask during the question and answer period.

Donation Information

Lastly, have donation forms, envelopes and jars available for people to donate to the Elder Speak Program.

Lesson 17

Volunteers

In life always treat others as you would like to be treated.
Then you will have happiness and peace in your life and in the hereafter – God Bless.

~ HELEN RAYFIELD

VOLUNTEERS ARE THE backbone of the Elder Speak Community Event.

The volunteers who meet and greet people as they arrive help create a sense of welcome and can answer any questions.

Volunteers who serve refreshments help people feel welcomed to partake of any food or drink you provide and keep the serving platters filled.

Ushers who help seat audience members, and later, the Elders, provide a sense of service and community.

Microphone runners who help take the microphone to audience members with questions provide personal attention to each person. We ask the audience to hold their questions until the last half of the program, after the Elders have all spoken. Then, as the lights are brought up in the audience, the runners can bring the microphone to anyone who has a question.

A crew to help with the setup and take down of tables, chairs, any promotional materials and donation jars is helpful and community building as well. If you are promoting this as a "by donation" event as we do, it is important to have convenient receptacles available where donations can be made.

Lesson 18

Technical Support

Kindness and respect for others brings happiness and peace.

~ FRANCIS COLLINS

TECHNICAL SUPPORT IS crucial in a large theater or if you choose to go live online. When Snowy Owl Theater was offered to us, technical support came with it. Eric Frank, the technician at the theater, has walked us through the use of microphones, lighting, filming, and online streaming options each year. It is an ever-changing and challenging opportunity. Having someone with technical knowledge is crucial to putting on a large event. If you are offered a large venue, ask about technical support: who you can talk to; who runs that aspect of the venue; and how they can help you with your event.

Another consideration is to provide online viewing for anyone who cannot make it to the day of the event. With an online viewing option, people can view it remotely and watch it at a later date as well.

Here are examples of technical support used for Elder Speak Community Events.
1. Microphones
   a. Handheld, three to four
   b. Lapel, four to five
2. Speakers
   a. On stage for the Elders to hear each other and the audience
   b. For the audience
3. Lighting
   a. Highlight the Elders and their setting
   b. Light the audience during question and answer segment

4. Streaming
    a. Stream the event on social media and/or YouTube
    b. Provide access to the stream after the event
5. Student film
    a. Stream the film to virtual audience
    b. Show film on a large screen to live audience
6. Film Event
    a. Record the event on film
    b. Provide each Elder with a flash drive of the film or provide the online link
    c. Put film of event on your website

The Elder Speak Community Event can be large or small. A smaller event may need less technical support and may feel more intimate. Research what your resources are and work with what you have. We often tell our Elders that if their wisdom connects with just one person, that is enough.

Lesson 19

Preparing Elders for the Elder Speak Community Event

When dealing with family or a mentee, wisdom is not continually directing, protecting or giving answers. Listen, encourage, allow dreams, and accept failures. Stress setting a goal not a path, but do not wander aimlessly. Have confidence in yourself – Persevere.

~ *JERRY GIBBONS*

YOU HAVE BEEN preparing the Elders for the community event since the beginning of the Elder Speak Program. Here is a breakdown showing some important aspects of before, during and after the event.

Rehearsal

The value of the rehearsal is the opportunity for Elders to experience being in conversation with one another in the venue. They meet the team that is supporting them and they become familiar with the schedule for day of the event.

Bring the Elders to the venue a few weeks before the community event. Let them get comfortable with the venue and meet their support team. Talk through the day of event timeline (see appendix) to help the Elders know what they can expect. Show them where they will wait before going into the theater and where they sit before going onstage. If there are stairs, make sure the Elders can navigate them. Find out who would like support from ushers getting to the stage. When they are on the stage, have the Elders practice sitting in their assigned chairs. Allow each Elder time to practice speaking into a microphone and engaging in answering questions and making conversation.

Day Before

Call each Elder and check in. Remind them of the event, time and location. Listen for any anxiety and visit with them until they are comfortable. Be sure you have their phone number or a person to call if something goes wrong and they are late for the event.

Day of the Event

Elders arrive one hour before the event starts. Have a space, apart from the general audience, where the Elders can rest and gather when they arrive. Let them relax, visit, look over their notes, use the restroom, and whatever else they need. Always have at least one facilitator with them.

The theater technician will need to attach their lapel microphones and test the volume. Prior to the program beginning, ushers will seat the Elders in the audience or on the stage, depending on how you decide to begin your program. If the Elders are seated in the audience, ushers will escort the Elders to their seats onstage when it's time.

Once the Elders are seated onstage, the facilitators introduce each one in turn and asks a deepening question about the wisdom statement of that Elder. This starts the ten minutes in which they share their life experience and the wisdom they have discovered. Keep track of time to maintain your schedule.

Facilitators sitting among the Elders during the event are there to support anyone who loses their place, rambles, or feels uncomfortable in any way. Questions that are hard to hear can be repeated and conversation can be encouraged among all the Elders. Elders are kept within their allotted time frame, which ensures that everyone gets an equal chance to talk.

After the Elders have all shared their wisdom, the program opens to a question-and-answer period with the audience. It helps the Elder if the facilitator repeats the questions from the audience. If a question is asked of the group and there is a long pause, re-ask the question to the Elder you think might best have the experience to answer. If there are no questions from the audience, the facilitators can ask the Elders questions. It may be worth preparing some in advance just in case.

After the Event

When the program is finished, ask the audience to remain seated while the ushers escort the Elders from the stage back to the room where they first gathered. Their microphones are removed and they collect their things. Now they can join family and friends gathered outside.

Lesson 20

Facilitator Preparation for Event

I believe the first wisdom is to know who I am.

~ Jim Telford

You HAVE BEEN preparing for the community event since the beginning of the Elder Speak Program. Here is a breakdown showing some important aspects of before and during the event.

Before:

1. Create the schedule of the day (see appendix).
2. Prior to the event, write out everything you plan to say. Practice these until they flow easily.
   * Your greetings to the audience
   * An introduction of the Elder Speak Program
   * Gratitude to sponsors
   * Encouragement for donations
   * Introductions for each Elder
   * Closing statements
3. The day before the event, check in with volunteers and with sponsors who are donating food and refreshments. Confirm what time they are arriving and if you need to pick anything up.

Day of the Event:

Review and follow the schedule for the event.

Have a timepiece available to help maintain the schedule throughout the program.

Before Elders and volunteers arrive, come together with your fellow facilitators in a quiet moment to focus on your purpose: supporting the unfolding and sharing of wisdom. Take a deep breath and feel support from and for each other and the spirit of the Elder Speak Program. Be aware of the beautiful journey you have all taken together with these Elders. Allow this beauty to carry you.

Now relax and enjoy yourself. You have been on an amazing journey with these Elders and your fellow facilitators. Enjoy this moment and take in all it has to offer. This is a precious time for you, the Elders and your community.

Lesson 21

After the Community Event

Knowledge is like a tool of one's trade,
and wisdom is the skill to use that knowledge.

~ EVERETT BURTS

THE TIME AFTER the event is as important as the time before and during. As with any journey, what was experienced needs to be acknowledged, reflected upon, and integrated into daily life.

Writing thank you notes:

Expressing gratitude to volunteers and those who provided financial and in-kind donations integrates them and their contributions into the Elder Speak Community Event. They learn how their contributions have strengthened the community and allowed each Elder to feel valued.

Final debriefing/meeting with Elders:

1. Arrange a meeting within two weeks of event
2. Share overall audience feedback with the Elders
3. Ask Elders for the feedback they received after the event
4. Ask Elders for their personal experience of the community event
   a. Ask for any difficulties the Elders had during the event
   b. Ask for any changes they might suggest that could improve the event
5. Ask the Elders how they use the experience of their Journey to Wisdom in their daily life

6. Explore ways to continue using the tools and insights they gained on their Journey to Wisdom
    a. Ask how this experience has affected their goals
    b. How has it affected their relationships with family and friends?
    c. How has this experienced affected their view of themselves?
    d. How did this experience affect their understanding of their family history?
    e. How do they see themselves moving forward in their lives with this new understanding?

Final Debriefing with Facilitators:

1. Ask what worked and what didn't
2. Ask what could have been done differently
3. Ask how each Elder benefited from the journey
4. Ask what each facilitator learned from their journey with the Elders

Appendix

Can you imagine millions
of strong-spirited,
free-thinking,
courageous Elders
living in our cities and towns?
It is my hope for the world.

~SAGE'S TAO TE CHING

Email template

Elder Speak 2022

Hi _____,

We are excited that you have expressed an interest in joining our Elder Speak Program. We have put together some information for you to read to help you understand the program.

What we are asking of you if you choose to join:

- Two zoom meetings per month (16 meetings) that would run from January 2022 through August 2022.
- Completion of a Wisdom Worksheet.
- An interview and filming of you with the high school students of a Digital Media class and their teacher, Eric Link.
- An interview with Rufus Woods and the publication of that in the Wenatchee World.
- Willingness to go on stage for the program Sunday, September 18 (possibly filmed without audience for a virtual event).

We invite you to watch the Elder Speak Program we presented in September of this year as a virtual event. You will find the replay of the event at this web link: https://youtu.be/47WCP7DJJIo

Thanks for considering joining Elder Speak,

(Your name)

An introduction to the Elder Speak Program by Deb Pobst.

With today's busy and often distracting environment, we are left to wonder: How do we instill our heritage of integrity, community and professionalism so that it resonates with and is carried forth by future generations?

Connecting generations is the vision of Elder Speak. For we know that when the wisdom and experience of Elders is brought forward into a community, it gives our community a broader base to stand on, a deeper strength to lean into, and more resiliency and understanding among its members.

Dave Notter was one of our 2020 Elders. This is his experience of being an Elder.

When I was asked to join Elder Speak as one of the Elders for 2020, I was initially ambivalent. I felt inadequate to offer any "wisdom" to others, and understood the program poorly. Was it a variation of a "support group", or of a "self-help" program? Or both? Or neither?

Well, now after finishing up with my cohort (the three other Elders, and the three Elder Speak facilitators who helped to guide us in our conversations twice per month during the year), I have clearer perspective: The program turned out to have very high personal value. It is neither a support group nor strictly a self-help group—it is basically a program in which four people with "long lives behind them" ("Elders") simply talk together in person, conversationally as a group, with occasional guidance from three facilitators for the program, about aspects of their cumulative life experiences, and about the meaning or impact coming from them. No syllabus, no presentations, no strict outline—just informal conversations and stories and personal examples, shared together. This unassuming format in fact has great power to allow insight or to amplify meanings from a person's remembered life events, as told to others by direct sharing.

Elder Speak is basically an "inward journey" for each participant—but is enabled by its external shared format. In the 9-month process, four people who begin mostly as strangers evolve to seem as family members; and each person gains insight and meaning—basically, "wisdom" —almost automatically in the process, by considering and sharing their individual stories and their own life experiences. We each came to know ourselves more deeply than before. So, we each discovered ourselves with "new eyes." This was a remarkable outcome.

I would recommend Elder Speak highly to anyone. It has great personal value.

Rufus Woods did interviews with each of our Elders both in written and podcast formats. Below is one of the written interviews.

Rev. Nancy Gradwohl reminds us to continue growing, learning, loving
BY RUFUS WOODS · PUBLISHED NOVEMBER 2, 2020 · UPDATED OCTOBER 29, 2020
Rev. Nancy Gradwohl, the pastor at Faith Lutheran in Leavenworth, is the kind of person who never stops learning, growing and evolving as a human being. She's comfortable in her own skin, speaks her mind and is unwilling to follow convention.

When she tells you that she got her first tattoo at age 50, took out a loan to attend seminary at age 71 and has done a variety of jobs from being a barmaid, retail clerk, seamstress and even a manure forker on the racetrack, it's apparent that she's full of life and is nowhere near done serving others.

Gradwohl, who is of Danish descent and grew up in Seattle, was one of four individuals who participated in the Ripple Foundation's Elder Speak program in September, joining Sandy Reiman, Dr. David Notter and Jim Telford.

During the year-long Elder Speak process, the group met regularly and reflected on life experiences, lessons learned and wisdom gained. I was particularly taken with Gradwohl's wisdom statement that emerged from those dialogues: "Everything comes from somewhere," which refers to the notion that people are a product of their experiences and environment and the importance of trying to understand why people do what they do rather than simply judge and write them off. This is a lesson that all of us could learn from and put into practice.

Gradwohl got interested in the Lutheran church as a young girl and once was invited to "preach a message," which she said was unusual for a female teenager. At that time, the Lutherans did not ordain women, so becoming a pastor wasn't an option.

After retiring from teaching middle school, she served as a lay pastoral assistant and was introduced to the experience of being with individuals who were in the process of dying, something she described as "a very nourishing experience" that included moments of tenderness and also moments of hilarity.

She recalled one such instance in which the woman was ready and prepared to transition from this life. Gradwohl visited and check to see if the woman was still breathing. The woman woke up with a start and said, "Oh, crap. It's you," and was disappointed she was still alive.

That story is vintage Nancy Gradwohl. She takes life as it comes and meets it with gusto.

During her time at Pacific Lutheran Theological Seminary in Berkeley, she recalled spending time engaging in a cross-cultural experience to engage people in different circumstances; it involved doing night ministry on the streets of San Francisco. "We went into communities that I had never imagined when I was in my 20s and 30s," Gradwohl told me.

They would be out from 9 p.m. until 2 a.m. and in the course of the work visited transgender and gay bars and talked to people living in alleys. "One young man could have been one of my sons," Gradwohl recalled. She gave him a pair of socks and he asked her to pray for him, "so I put my hand on his shoulder and I prayed," she said.

She had rich conversations with people who were struggling in life but who were still human beings. "So, I learned a lot about my attitude and the caste system (in this country)," Gradwohl said. She sees how difficult life is for people on the margins and bristles at the attitude some express that these folks should go out and get a job. "That really makes me mad when people are condescending," Gradwohl told me. How are they supposed to get a job when they haven't bathed, don't have clean clothes, aren't sure how to fill out a job application, etc., she said. "They don't have a support system and maybe they haven't had for years," she added. This deep sense of compassion and an unwillingness to write people off led her to the ministry.

At 81, she's not slowing down. "I don't feel like my life is over. I feel like my life is just a big adventure and I don't know what's around the corner," she said.

As a society, she thinks we should choose to be kind, treat others with respect and dignity, and abandon the rampant materialism and selfishness that drive our culture. Nancy Gradwohl is helping us see the humanity in others, and we need that these days.

Sample Donation Request

Your logo here

(Date here)

Dear Committee Members,

We want to thank you for your strong support of (Your Organizations Name Here) Elder Speak over the past____ years.

As you may know, (Your Organizations Name Here) (Your website here) is a local nonprofit. Our vision is: *"A world of compassionate connections."* Our Elder Speak program strives to fulfill that vision by creating an oral and visual history of esteemed Elders from our community. Each year four Elders volunteer to take the Elder Speak journey. These four Elders, under the guidance of Elder Speak program managers _____and _____, will explore, reveal, reflect, and share their life and wisdom. This journey is more than just story telling. Over the course of nine months, a deep and meaningful process emerges not only for the Elders, but their families and ultimately their community.

Wisdom is a very human experience, born from our experiences. It is that golden nugget that informs us in times of need. Elder Speak is the opportunity for us to learn the wisdom of our Elders.

To capture the journey, (Your Organization here) has partnered with the students at the _____ class. These young adults film, interview, edit and produce a 20-minute film that is shown at our annual Elder Speak community event held at (Your venue here) in September.

This year our esteemed elders are (Name Elders here).

We hope that you are inspired to help Elder Speak continue to make a difference in the lives of our community members by supporting our efforts with your sponsorship of $_____.

Your gift will be immediately put to work to grow the foundation and propel its impact to the community. Corporate sponsors are the support structure that allows the foundation to operate professionally, deliver clear messaging and promotion, cover operating expenses and extend our arms to the community.

You will receive: Placement of company logo or name at the event, logo on a slide presentation during the event, display of logo on welcome table and on most media material in addition to group social media posts.

Sincerely and in gratitude,

_____Program Managers

_____Executive Director

_____Board President

Sample Lesson for Elder Speak in a School Classroom

The school lesson is a lesson plan that brings Elders and students together so that students can interact with Elders to hear their stories and wisdom. Students then reflect back the stories and wisdom that has personal meaning to them through art, film, writing, or some other means of communication.

The Lesson Plan

Four years ago, Roselyn Robison, a local high school English teacher, invited us to explain to her students about Elder Speak and how we interview Elders to correspond with a Native American lesson she teaches that includes sitting with an Elder to hear their stories. Students then share the story in film, poetry, art, or in some other artistic form. Roselyn generously shared her lesson plan for this manual. You will find it below.

Wisdom Worksheet for Teens

When we met with Roselyn's class, we brought a Wisdom Worksheet with us that was designed for teens. After they complete the worksheet, students break into pairs to share their story with one another and what they learned from it. They also get the opportunity to share their wisdom. Then, once the class is brought back together, each student has a chance to share a wisdom they heard without telling who they learned it from. You will find the Teen Wisdom Worksheet below.

✍

Sample Teacher Lesson Plan

The purpose of this assignment is to encourage two traditions we have been learning about in class: the art of oral tradition and a deep respect for one's Elders. For this assignment (which is summative), you will interview your family's "storyteller"—this could be parents or a grandparent; it could be an aunt—who in your family is responsible for holding the family "stories"? Record or take good notes during the interview—this interview will be more effective if done face-to-face, but, if necessary, it can be conducted via a phone call. Do not interview via text or email!!! You can use the suggested questions or come up with your own. Follow the guidelines learned in class. After the interview, your job will be to share the stories you learn with the class and to create a visual/written record of what was said. This is a class assignment, but you might think of this as a way to make sure the valuable stories of your Elders are kept safe and will be accessible for future generations.

Step One: Learn and Take Notes

Notes - The Art of the Interview

Step Two: Prepare

Select or write questions to use during the interview. Here are some ideas to get you started:

1. What is your full name? Why did your parents select this name for you? Did you have a nickname?
2. When and where were you born?
3. How did your family come to live there?
4. Were there other family members in the area? Who?
5. What was the house (apartment, farm, etc.) like? How many rooms? Bathrooms? Did it have electricity? Indoor plumbing? Telephones?
6. Were there any special items in the house that you remember?
7. What is your earliest childhood memory?
8. Describe the personalities of your family members.
9. What kind of games did you play growing up?
10. What was your favorite toy and why?
11. What was your favorite thing to do for fun (movies, beach, etc.)?
12. Did you have family chores? What were they? Which was your least favorite?
13. Did you receive an allowance? How much? Did you save your money or spend it?

14. What was school like for you as a child? What were your best and worst subjects? Where did you attend grade school? High school? College?
15. What school activities and sports did you participate in?
16. Do you remember any fads from your youth? Popular hairstyles? Clothes?
17. Who were your childhood heroes?
18. What were your favorite songs and music?
19. Did you have any pets? If so, what kind and what were their names?
20. What was your religion growing up? What church, if any, did you attend?
21. Were you ever mentioned in a newspaper?
22. Who were your friends when you were growing up?
23. What world events had the most impact on you while you were growing up? Did any of them personally affect your family?
24. Describe a typical family dinner. Did you all eat together as a family? Who did the cooking? What were your favorite foods?
25. How were holidays (birthdays, Christmas, etc.) celebrated in your family? Did your family have special traditions?
26. How is the world today different from what it was like when you were a child?
27. Who was the oldest relative you remember as a child? What do you remember about them?
28. What do you know about your family surname?
29. Is there a naming tradition in your family, such as always giving the firstborn son the name of his paternal grandfather?
30. What stories have come down to you about your parents? Grandparents? More distant ancestors?
31. Are there any stories about famous or infamous relatives in your family?
32. Have any recipes been passed down to you from family members?
33. Are there any physical characteristics that run in your family?
34. Are there any special heirlooms, photos, bibles or other memorabilia that have been passed down in your family?
35. What was the full name of your spouse? Siblings? Parents?
36. When and how did you meet your spouse? What did you do on dates?
37. What was it like when you proposed (or were proposed to)? Where and when did it happen? How did you feel?
38. Where and when did you get married?
39. What memory stands out the most from your wedding day?
40. How would you describe your spouse? What do (did) you admire most about them?
41. What do you believe is the key to a successful marriage?
42. How did you find out you were going to be a parent for the first time?
43. Why did you choose your children's names?
44. What was your proudest moment as a parent?
45. What did your family enjoy doing together?
46. What was your profession and how did you choose it?

47. If you could have had any other profession what would it have been? Why wasn't it your first choice?
48. Of all the things you learned from your parents, which do you feel was the most valuable?
49. What accomplishments were you most proud of?
50. What is the one thing you most want people to remember about you?

Step Three: Conduct Your Interview

Set aside time for this interview. Take notes as you interview OR record the interview and then add notes. Select 10 questions to focus on and let the magic happen.

My Question	Their Response:
1.	
2.	

3.

4.

5.

6.

7.	
8.	
9.	
10.	

Other Notes:

Step Four: Memorialize the Interview

After the interview, it is your job to create a lasting document/art/video/etc. to keep this information intact for future generations. This cannot just be a typed version of the interview. It is your job to immortalize the stories that were shared with you. Here are some ideas:

- Videotape the interview, cut and splice the video to create a coherent, memorable version of your Elder's story.
- Create a piece of art that includes/expresses the stories that were shared.
- Create an electronic presentation capturing the gist of the interview—this could be an infographic, a PowerPoint, etc.
- Create a written, coherent story about your Elder using the interview as inspiration.

If you have some other creative idea, please see Miss Robison for approval before moving forward.

Step Five: Share Your Project and Experience with the Class

During an informal story-telling circle, you will share the following:

- Who did you interview? Why did you select them?
- What two questions/answers stood out the most to you? Why?
- What is something you learned about your Elder/family history that you didn't know before?
- How did you choose to immortalize their story?
  - ◆ Show us your project
  - ◆ Why did you choose this format?
  - ◆ Explain the elements that you included and explain why each element is present.
- What will you do to ensure this valuable story continues to be told to future generations?

Timeline:

- Assignment Given: _____
- Interview Completed: _____
- Project Work Time: _____
- Share-Out Circle: _____
- Project & Paperwork Due: _____

Grading

A	Student has put forth their absolute best effort in all aspects of this assignment
B	Student has put forth a good effort in most aspects of this assignment
C	Student has put forth some effort in most aspects of this assignment
D	Students has put forth a good effort in most aspects of this assignment
F	Student needs to put forth more effort in all aspects of this assignment

Sample Teen Wisdom Worksheet

TEEN WISDOM WORKSHEET

Reflecting on your childhood, let us say, before 10 years of age, can you pinpoint any experience (positive or negative) that left a significant impression on you?

_____

_____

What, if anything, did you learn from this experience that has impacted your life?

_____

_____

Reflecting on your life up to now, can you identify any major experience (positive or negative) that left a significant impression on you?

_____

_____

Did any major learning occur because of this experience? If so, what was it?

_____

_____

Identify any additional experiences that left major lasting impressions.

_____

_____

What did these experiences teach you?

_____

_____

Now review your learnings (in bold print) above, and see if you can synthesize some or all of them in one or two WISDOM STATEMENTS, and write it/them below.

NOTE: Your WISDOM STATEMENT can be one or two short sentences.

ELDER SPEAK

Connecting Generations

We're Glad You're Here
Please enjoy our food and drink; it is welcome in the Theatre

4:00p We Begin
Drew Zabrocki, Board President
Steve Stroud, Executive Director, The Ripple Foundation

Our Facilitators
Deb Pobst & Theresa D-Litzenberger

Our Elders
Jan Wallick, Francis Collins,
Jerry Gibbons and Helen Rayfield
A Discussion
After the video and short stories we invite you to ask questions, share thoughts, and engage
in open conversation.

Thank you
Refreshments and social time will follow.
Your tax-deductible financial contribution may be made today in support of
The Ripple Foundation

Our deepest gratitude to the community for the broad range of support including contributions from:

Anonymous Donors, Eagle Creek Winery, Icicle Creek Center for the Arts, NCW Life, Wenatchee Valley
Technical Skills Center, Dan's Food Market, Cashmere Valley Bank

Sample Program B side 1

Sunday, September 19th, 2021

**We're Glad You're Here
Please enjoy our food and drink;
it is welcome in the Theatre**

4:00 We Begin
Steve Stroud, *Executive Director*
The Ripple Foundation

Facilitators
**Deb Pobst, Robin Boal
& Theresa D-Litzenberger**

Elders
**Jan Wallick, Francis Collins,
Jerry Gibbons and Helen Rayfield**

A Discussion
**After the video and short stories, we invite you to ask questions, share thoughts, and engage
in open conversation.**

Thank you
**Refreshments and social time will follow.
Your tax-deductible financial contribution may be made today in support of the
Ripple Foundation.**

Our deepest gratitude to our community for the broad range
of support including contributions from:

*Anonymous donors Cashmere Valley Bank, Dan's Food Market, Eagle Creek Winery, Icicle Creek Center
for the Arts, Wenatchee Valley Technical Skills Center*

Sample Program B side 2

Wisdom Statements

Kindness and respect for others brings happiness and peace.

~ FRANCIS COLLINS

When dealing with family or a mentee wisdom is not continually directing, protecting or giving answers. Listen, encourage, allow dreams, accept failures. Stress setting a goal not a path, but do not wander aimlessly. Have confidence in yourself – Persevere.

~ JERRY GIBBONS

In life always treat others as you would like to be treated. Then you will have happiness and peace in your life and in the hereafter – God Bless.

~ HELEN RAYFIELD

Things don't always go as planned. You have to accept change.

~ JAN WALLICK

Notes

_____

_____

_____

_____

Sample Schedule

Elder Speak 2018 Sample Day of Event Schedule for Facilitators

11:30   Team Brief and Meet to Commence Setup

11:45   **Volunteers:** Set up Stage, Tables, Banners and Décor Items

- **Program manager:** Give PowerPoint to tech to run in the lobby on a loop (PowerPoint will be programmed to loop)
- **Program manager:** Give tech thumb drive of student video to play, David test video (if he hasn't gotten this beforehand)

If possible, PowerPoint and thumb drive are sent to David days ahead of time along with a picture of Sponsor logo

1:00   **Elders Arrive**

Volunteers Arrive

Volunteer: Donation jars set up

Ushers: Four if needed

Food Prep & Service Volunteers

Wine Server: Winery server

Volunteer: Registration– program manager provides what is needed for registration

1. Programs
2. Signup sheet
3. Cashbox
4. Pens

Volunteer: Sponsor Table– program manager provides what is needed for Sponsor table.

1. Pamphlets
2. Upcoming events
3. Business cards
4. Flyers

Program Manager: - post banquet permit

Food and Drink will be picked up by volunteer (arrive at 1:15)

Volunteers set up and serve food and refreshments

| 1:15 | **Program manager**: Mic Set-up for Elders / Elders comfortably wait in the Green Room or on Stage |

1:15 · **Program manager**: Mic Set-up for Elders / Elders comfortably wait in the Green Room or on Stage
- 4 Elders with Lapel Mics, We will have each of them talk to get the levels set
- 2 Wireless Stage Mic for Facilitators
- 2 Wireless Mic for Runner (volunteers)

Music – Tech will take care of this
Tech: Start power point Slide Show on Lobby TV
Volunteer: Registration Opens
Program Manager: Information Area
Wine Server: Bartender/Server in Place

1:50 · **Program manager**: Makes announcement in lobby and informs everyone that it's time to head in
Tech: Start Audio and Video Recording
- Two Angles; one fixed on all Elders all the time and the other directed at the person speaking

Music Changes
Ushers: direct people to their seats
Mic Runners will take a seat near front on each side of theater
Elders are seated in the auditorium

2:00 · **Program manager** welcomes everyone to Elder Speak. Talks about his experience with Elder Speak. Introduces Executive Director.

2:05 · **Executive Director** Introduces Sponsor and gives a general introduction to Elder Speak.

2:10 · **Executive Director** introduces **Program managers**

2:15 · **Program Managers** each talk about Elder speak and their connection to it.

2:20 · **Program manager** introduces student video
Student Video plays

2:40 · Elders brought onstage. (ushers help)
Program manager introduce Elders
Program manager Facilitate Conversation

3:20 or so · Questions from children first and then from audience

3:50 · **Executive Director** Closing Remarks. Ask ushers to come up to escort Elders to Green Room
Usher assists Elders from the stage – Elders go to Green Room

4:00-4:30 · Social gathering
4:30-5:00 · Break Down

Sample Elder Day of Event Schedule

Elder Speak 2021 – Elders Day of Event Schedule

Snowy Owl Theater

September 19, 3:00-6:30 pm

3:00- Arrive and meet on patio at Snowy Owl Theater. We will go to the green room and you can leave your things there.

3:15- Ushers are introduced and take you to the stage where each person is fitted with a microphone. We will return to green room until it's time for ushers to take you in for the program.

3:45- Go to seats in the theater – ushers will show you the way.

4:00- Program begins. Welcome and introductions to program, then the student film is shown.

4:30- Robin introduces each Elder as you come on stage. Ushers will assist.

4:35- Each Elder takes a turn (10 min.) sharing life experience and wisdom gained.

Deb, Theresa and Robin may interject questions to deepen.

5:10- Questions from the audience. Mic runners and panel will assist. We will repeat questions so you can hear them as needed.

5:50- Closing statements by Steve Stroud.

6:00- Elders, ushers will assist you back to green room. Mics will be removed in the green room.

Mingle with friends and family outside on the patio and enjoy yourselves.

Thank you. You can leave whenever you'd like.

Sample Photo Release Form A

Your Logo Here

RELEASE WAIVER

For good and valuable consideration, the receipt and sufficiency of which is hereby acknowledged, I, the undersigned, agree as follows:

1. I agree to be photographed, recorded and videotaped by (<u>Your Organization here</u>) and its agent, (<u>Name of school</u>) and (<u>Name of venue</u>), in connection with my participation in Elder Speak (event) on September 19. 2021.

2. I hereby irrevocably authorize (<u>Your Organization here</u>) and its affiliates to copyright, publish, reproduce, exhibit, transmit, broadcast, televise, digitize, display, otherwise use, and permit others to use, (a) my name, image, likeness, and voice, and (b) all photographs, recordings, videotapes, audiovisual materials, writings, statements, and quotations of or by myself (collectively, the "Materials"), in any manner, form, or format whatsoever now or hereinafter created, including on the Internet, and for any purpose, including, but not limited to, advertising or promotion of (<u>Your Organization here</u>), its affiliates, or their services, without further consent from or payment to me.

3. It is understood that all of the Materials, and all films, audiotapes, videotapes, reproductions, media, plates, negatives, photocopies, and electronic and digital copies of the Materials, are the sole property of (<u>Your Organization here</u>). I agree not to contest the rights or authority granted to (<u>Your Organization here</u>) hereunder. I hereby forever release and discharge (<u>Your Organization here</u>), its employees, licensees, agents, successors, and assigns from any claims, actions, damages, liabilities, costs, or demands whatsoever arising by reason of defamation, invasion of privacy, right of publicity, copyright infringement, or any other personal or property rights from or related to any use of the Materials. I understand that (<u>Your Organization here</u>) is under no obligation to use the Materials.

4. This document contains the entire agreement between (<u>Your Organization here</u>) and the undersigned concerning the subject matter hereof.

Date: _____   _____

                                                   Signature of Participant

                                                   _____

                                                   Name of Participant

Sample Photo Release Form B

Photo Release Form

Your Logo Here

I, _____, give my permission to use my name, likeness, image, voice, and/or appearance as such may be embodied in any pictures, photos, video recordings, audiotapes, digital images, and the like, taken or made on behalf of (<u>Your Organization here</u>) during any event, workshop, class, retreat, or function. I understand these photos may be used in a wide variety of promotional materials including, but not limited to, newsletters, flyers, posters, brochures, advertisements, broadcast public service advertising (PSAs), fundraising letters, annual reports, press releases, (<u>Your Organization here</u>) website, (<u>Your Organization here</u>) social networking sites and other print and digital communications of (<u>Your Organization here</u>).

I have read and understand the above:

Signature _____

Printed name _____ Date _____

Sample Wisdom Worksheet

WISDOM WORKSHEET

Reflecting on your childhood, let us say, up to about 10 years of age, can you pinpoint any experience (positive or negative) that left a significant impression on you?

_____

_____

What, if anything, did you learn from this experience that has lasted through your life or a major part of it?

_____

_____

Reflecting on your life as a teenager, can you identify any major experience (positive or negative) that left a significant impression on you?

_____

_____

Did any major learning occur because of this experience? If so, what was it?

_____

_____

Reflecting on your life roughly from 20-55, can you identify any major experience(s) that left a lasting memory?

_____

_____

What did you learn from this?

_____

_____

Identify any additional experiences that left major lasting impressions.

_____

_____

What did these experiences teach you?

_____

_____

Now review your learnings (**in bold print**) above, and see if you can synthesize some or all of them in one or two WISDOM STATEMENTS, and write it/them below

_____

_____

NOTE: Your WISDOM STATEMENT can be one or two short sentences.

Sample Introduction/Discussion Topics for Event

2021 Event Introductions

Francis Collin's life journey began in Ireland, where he was born and raised in a military camp originally built during the Crimean War, and was the youngest of four boys in high school. Francis was taught by Dominican priests, an important part of his life experience. At one time, Francis wanted to be an oceanographer but ultimately chose dentistry, then, ever the learner, added schooling to be a medical doctor and a surgeon. He came to the United States to work in Texas and ended up staying in this country to work in Seattle, and finally, in Wenatchee, his home for many years.

Throughout the year of looking at his life journey, Francis always came back to how important kindness and respect has been to him. Francis's wisdom statement is: **Kindness and respect bring happiness and peace.**

I love the image Francis shared of his mother cleaning graffiti off a neighbor's wall in the early morning. He often talks of how both his Father and Mother talked about and demonstrated accepting others. Francis, please tell our audience: What were the experiences and the feeling in your home and community that impacted you so deeply that it inspired your wisdom statement? How does kindness and respect for others, which brings happiness and peace, relate to our community today?

Helen Rayfield's life journey brought her from Tennessee to Leavenworth as a child, where she has lived, raised a family, worked and played her entire life. She contributes so much to the community to this day. Through her business, The Big Y, Helen provided a place for orchardists to gather daily, families to share meals, and for teenagers to work and be mentored.

One thing Helen said that struck me is that she shared so much with this Elder Speak group that we may know more about her than people who have known her for many years. She has been so open and honest with us throughout the year. It is Helen's way to be open and truthful, we found.

Helen's wisdom statement is: **In life always treat others as you would like to be treated. Then you will have happiness and peace in your life and in the hereafter. God Bless**

This reminds me of the Golden Rule. Do unto others as you would have them do unto you. I'm curious, how do people do that? Please tell the audience an example from your life where you were treated as you wanted to be treated. How did that change your life?

Do you have an example of when you were not treated well? How did you handle that?

What are some reflections you have for how people can treat one another when there is disagreement in how to think?

Sample Elder Speak Program Checklist/Timeline for the Year

Elder Speak Timeline

October-December:

- Confirm Elders
- Meet and greet with Elders
- Hand out Wisdom Worksheet
- Schedule interviews of Elders with high school media arts class
- Film Elders at high school media arts class

January:

- Meet with Elders twice – start telling individual life stories
- Collect signed permission forms for photos
- Collect biographies
- Take individual photos
- Post about program/share about Elders on website
- Find venue for the Elder Speak Community Event and confirm date
- Begin securing financial sponsorships

February:

- Meet with Elders twice – complete telling individual life stories
- Secure financial sponsorships
- Contact newspaper and schedule interviews of Elders to start in May

March:

- Meet with Elders twice
- Begin general discussions with Elders
- Work with Wisdom Worksheets

April:

- Meet with Elders twice
- Continue general discussions with Elders
- Work with Wisdom Worksheets
- Check in with high school film class about progress of film
- Confirm the schedule of interviews dates and times with the newspaper

May:

- Meet with Elders twice
- Start to zero in on the Elders' wisdom statements
- Newspaper interview of first Elder takes place and is published in May
- Confirm in-kind donations of food and drinks for event
- Search for volunteers for the event

June:

- Meet with Elders twice
- Continue zeroing in on the wisdom statements in discussions
- Newspaper interview of second Elder takes place and is published in June
- Reconfirm event venue, date and time
- Create save-the-date postcards
- Post on social media

July:

- Meet with Elders twice
- Continue zeroing in on wisdom statements in discussions
- Post event on social media
- Print save-the-date postcards, posters and flyers.
- If putting flyers with Chamber of Commerce newsletter, arrange for this.
- Newspaper interview of third Elder takes place and is published in July

August:

Elders:

1. Meet with Elders twice
2. Confirm Elders' wisdom statements
3. Newspaper interview of fourth Elder takes place and is published in August
4. Hand out day-of-event schedule
5. Answer questions, support Elders in whatever way they need
6. Hand out save-the-date postcards to give to friends and family
7. Schedule a September practice date at venue

Staff:

1. Create two schedules of the day of event. One for Elders, one for staff.
2. Hand out day-of-event schedule to staff
3. Mail postcards at the beginning of the month
4. Put up posters and flyers toward the middle of the month
5. Post on social media once or twice a week
6. Email reminders to supporters
7. Meet with venue staff to confirm event needs
8. Print programs for event

9. Secure film from high school media class
10. Confirm volunteers
11. Confirm all in-kind donations
12. Schedule with venue a practice run through with Elders in September

September:

Elders:

1. Rehearsal at the venue

    a. Seating arrangements
    b. Speaking order
    c. Review schedule of the day
    d. Speaking into microphones
    e. Practice talking to the audience and to one another on the stage

2. Answer questions, support Elders in whatever way they need

Staff:

1. Refine day of schedule, last minute changes, etc.
2. Continue to post on social media and email people
3. Call Elders the day before the event to check in and confirm the time they will arrive at the venue.
4. Take student film to tech support at venue at least one day before the event
5. Do whatever is necessary to prepare and decorate the stage for the event

Day of Event:

1. Prepare/deliver refreshments
2. Meet and greet volunteers before the event begins and answer any questions about their responsibilities
3. Check in with tech support at venue
4. Meet Elders and follow day of schedule
5. Enjoy doing the event
6. Clean up and break down after the event

After Event:

1. Check in with the Elders
2. Write thank you notes for any donations received
3. Write thank you notes to sponsors
4. Schedule a meeting with Elders to talk about the event and their experience
5. Ask for any suggestions the Elders might have to improve the event
6. Thank the Elders for taking this Heroic Journey to Wisdom

List of Event Volunteer Responsibilities

1. Set up room where people will gather before and after the Elder Speak Community Event
   a. Set up tables and chairs where people might gather
   b. Set out flowers
   c. Set out donation jars
   d. Set up any tables with promotional materials
2. Set up stage
   a. Set up chairs, tables, drinking glasses, water
   b. Set out flowers
   c. Create ambiance
3. Registration
   a. Set up table and chair
   b. Set out programs, signup sheet, donation box or jar, list of people already signed up
   c. Pens or pencils
   d. Flowers
   e. Greet each person as they arrive
   f. Have people sign in
   g. Direct them to take a pen or pencil with them to use to write on the program if they want
4. Food and Drink
   a. Make platters if not already made
   b. Set out platters on tables
   c. Set out napkins, eating utensils and plates if needed
   d. Make coffee and tea water
   e. Set out cups, sugar and cream, honey, tea bags
   f. Set up water and glasses
   g. Refresh platters
   h. Refresh coffee and hot water
5. Wine
   a. Set up wine bar with wine and glasses
   b. Serve wine
   c. Set up donation jar on wine table
   d. Have a table or glass holder available for used wine glasses
   e. Clean up afterward
6. Ushers
   a. Guide people into the theater as needed
   b. Guide Elders to their seats

    c. Guide Elders onto stage as needed

    d. Guide Elders off stage as needed

7. Microphone Runners

    a. Get a microphone from tech

    b. Sit on one side of the theater opposite the second runner

    c. Go to a person who raises a hand during question and answer period

    d. Give the person a microphone and let the question be asked

    e. Retrieve the microphone and repeat the question the person asked

    f. Continue until time is up or no one raises a hand

    g. Return microphone to tech

List of Needed Items for Elder Speak Community Event

1. Food
2. Utensils, tablecloths, serving plates, napkins
3. Cups, glasses, wine glasses
4. Drinks (coffee, tea, water)
5. Wine
6. Tables and chairs
7. Stage furniture
8. Flowers
9. Garbage/Recycle bins
10. Programs
11. Registration materials
12. Promotional material
13. Power point, film on flash drive
14. Donation jars
15. Thank you cards and gifts for Elders

Acknowledgments

We are grateful to every Elder who has participated in the Elder Speak Program. They have inspired us with their courage and willingness to deeply explore life experiences. They have gifted us with their wisdom. Thank you for sharing that wisdom at the Elder Speak Community Event. It has been an honor to be on this Journey with each of you.

A special thank you to Icicle Creek Center for the Arts for contributing the beautiful Snowy Owl Theater for each Community Event, and to Rebecca Ryker and Eric Frank in particular. You gave us a home base and unflagging technical support. Thank you.

Thank you to The Ripple Foundation for sponsoring the Elder Speak Program and for the tireless guidance and support of Steve Stroud, Executive Director, and the steadfast support of the Board of Directors, particularly past Board President Drew Zabrocki and past Secretary/Treasurer Sarah Zabrocki.

We are deeply grateful to Robin Boal for joining us as a facilitator, note taker extraordinaire, and wise friend. This is a better program because of you. Also, thank you to Rufus Woods, Publisher Emeritus of the Wenatchee World, for interviewing the Elders each year, highlighting Elder Speak in the local newspaper and being one of our greatest supporters. We give special thanks to Eric Link and his media classes. Eric and the students have given hours and hours of their time toward creating insightful films of the Elders. Each year they welcome us into their classroom for thoughtful and engaging interviews that support the Elders in their Journey.

We have had many Sponsors over the years, and we are grateful for their continued support: Cashmere Valley Bank, Dan's Food Market, Icicle Creek Center for the Arts, Eagle Creek Winery, Roots, and Mountain Meadows Senior Living Center.

We want to thank all the volunteers who help during the Community Event. This Event could not happen without your support. And to our community, thank you for your support and donations. You have come to witness our Elders as they share their lives and wisdom. And you have laughed, cried, asked questions, and learned with us. Thank you.

To Morgan Fraser, editor, volunteer, and emotional supporter, thank you. Your editing skills have made this manual come to life. Thank you, Barbee Teasley, for your artistic skills creating our cover. You worked with us with an open heart and equanimity which made the cover selection easy for us. And to our husbands, Richard and Dennis. Thank you for your support while we spent days, months—well actually, years—on this project.

Selected Bibliography

Brooks, David *Nine Nonobvious Ways to have Deeper Conversations* New York Times. November 19, 2020

Cameron, Julia *The Listening Path* New York. St. Martin's Essentials. 2021

Chittester, Joan *The Gift of Years* New York. Bluebridge Books. 2008

Hoblitzelle, Olivia Ames *Aging with Wisdom* New York. Monkfish Books. 2017

Martin, William *The Sage's Tao Te Ching* New York. The Experiment. 2000

Murphy, Kate *You're Not Listening* New York. Celedon Books. 2020

Nepo, Mark *The Book of Awakening* San Francisco. Conari Press, 2011

Palmer, Parker *On The Brink of Everything* California. Berret-Kohler. 2018

Rabbi Rachel Cowan and Dr. Linda Thal *Wise Aging* New Jersey. Behrman House. 2015

Stroud, Steve ND, LAc *Quest* Steve Stroud 2019

About the Authors

Debbie Jo Pobst

Growing up in a remote farming community on the South Fork of the Nooksack River, Washington, Deb roamed free as a child. Her Elder neighbors, Tom, George, and Johnnie Nesset became the most important influences in her life. They shared their life wisdom freely through stories, and by example. This created the foundation that guided Deb toward Elder Speak.

Deb earned a Bachelor's of Science from the Barbara Brennan School of Healing, studied Transformational Breath, ran a healing practice for 10 years, and volunteered for 5 years at Little Bear, working with the Elders of the Lummi Nation. She is a founding member of The Ripple Foundation.

Deb lives in Plain, Washington with her husband Dennis. They have two grown children, three grandchildren, a dog, cat, horse and burro. Deb loves hiking, skiing, gardening, reading, being part of the Elder Speak Journey, and best of all, her grandchildren Chlo, Conan, and Juan.

Theresa D-Litzenberger

Theresa was born and raised in Michigan and moved to Leavenworth, Washington in 1980 to live in a historical log house in the mountains. She married Richard two years later. Together they opened a bakery alongside their home, using a 7-ton masonry oven in which to bake so that Theresa could live her passion for bread baking.

Twenty-two years later, Theresa began a new adventure attending Barbara Brennan School of Healing for four years and received her Certificate of Healing. Simultaneously, she worked at the local independent bookstore until 2020. In those years, she joined as staff The Ripple Foundation. Together with Deb Pobst, Theresa began the Elder Speak Program.

For More Information

If you would like to learn more information about the Elder Speak Program, please visit *www.theripplefoundation.org/elder-speak*. You can also contact us at info@theripplefoundation.com.